STATES OF INCARCERATION

FIELD NOTES

SERIES EDITOR: Paul Mattick

A series of books providing in-depth analyses of today's global turmoil as it unfolds. Each book focuses on an important feature of our present-day economic, political and cultural condition, addressing local and international issues. Field Notes examines the many dimensions of today's social predicament and provides a radical, politically and critically engaged voice to global debates.

Published in association with the *Brooklyn Rail*

STATES OF INCARCERATION

Rebellion, Reform, and America's Punishment System

JARROD SHANAHAN and ZHANDARKA KURTI

REAKTION BOOKS

This book is dedicated to everyone who walked the walk in the summer of 2020

Published by Reaktion Books Ltd
Unit 32, Waterside
44–48 Wharf Road
London N1 7UX, UK
www.reaktionbooks.co.uk

First published 2022
Copyright © Jarrod Shanahan and Zhandarka Kurti 2022

Printed and bound in Great Britain
by T. J. Books Ltd, Padstow, Cornwall

A catalogue record for this book is available from the British Library

ISBN 978 1 78914 666 0

Contents

Introduction:
A Moment of Promise and Pitfalls

Kenosha, Wisconsin, August 2020. An angry crowd gathered outside the Kenosha County Courthouse, 40 miles south of Milwaukee. The August heat chafed against face masks worn as much to guard against the COVID-19 pandemic, presently in full swing, as the tear gas and to protect identities from the prying camera lenses of ubiquitous photographers and live-streamers whose images have aided police in prosecuting protesters coast to coast. The previous day the Kenosha Police had shot Jacob Blake, a young Black man, while his children looked on, leaving him paralyzed from the waist down. Such shootings are a daily phenomenon in the United States, where state violence is delivered casually, and even celebrated in popular culture and the tabloid press as the necessary work of maintaining law and order in a land that never really ceased to be frontier. This is especially true in working-class communities of color like the one Blake called home, where cops saturate daily reality. Some young people grow up dreaming not of fighting back against the police, but of becoming one of them, joining the toughest gang in town and enjoying the safety and perquisites that come with meting out the violent compulsion at the core of capitalist society. But in the summer of 2020, a critical mass of working-class Americans chose to fight back, led by the Black residents of places like Kenosha.

Since the end of May, much of the United States had been the scene of the largest rebellion since the 1960s. Sparked by the police murder of George Floyd in Minneapolis, and exacerbated by the deaths of Breonna Taylor in Louisville, Kentucky, and Rayshard Brooks in Atlanta, Georgia, the George Floyd Rebellion set a new precedent for dealing with police murder: attacks on police and court infrastructure, including cars, stations, and even the cops themselves, alongside widespread looting and property destruction. In a year when "the new normal" became a cliché, a riotous response to police murder became just that. And in August 2020, as Jacob Blake lay in a hospital bed, only the latest victim in a string of atrocities that "police reform" cannot do anything to change, the people of Kenosha decided that immediate action must be taken.

Their primary target was the Kenosha County Courthouse. Almost immediately following Blake's shooting, an angry crowd graffitied and attempted to breach the building, most likely to set it on fire, as had been done to the Third Precinct in Minneapolis. Molotov cocktails briefly set the courthouse walls alight. Garbage trucks repurposed as barricades by the Kenosha Police were similarly ignited. The courthouse facade was spray-painted "Fuck 12," an anti-police slogan, alongside "Be water, spread fire," a reference to a global set of riot tactics initially associated with the 2019 rebellion in Hong Kong. Repelled by riot cops, the crowd hit the streets, smashing retailers' windows, setting a car dealership aflame, and looting whatever they could under the cover of darkness. The cops hung back to guard the supposed halls of justice, a detested symbol of the American punishment system.

The following night, a larger crowd came back for another shot at the courthouse, which was now heavily fortified, including a protective security fence the likes of which were springing up around carceral infrastructure across the United States. Riot cops sprayed tear gas, lobbed stun grenades, and fired rubber bullets at close range, as protesters responded with rocks, bottles, and fireworks. The crowd fought hard, but the courthouse was well protected by riot cops armed to the teeth with every imaginable tool of repression. Repelled from the courthouse, a rowdy march took off into the night, snaking through Kenosha's streets, knocking over light posts, smashing up some businesses and vehicles, and leaving others well enough alone, until it arrived at the Community Corrections building. "Get the PO!" someone yelled, meaning probation officer. "Oh shit," another rejoined, "they're getting the PO!" As one group smashed the facade of the building and attempted to enter, another produced spray cans and scrawled graffiti on the building's walls. One message proved particularly significant: "Abolish!"

Abolish! This terse command is the watchword of abolitionism, a popular political tendency calling for the eradication of police and prisons that had largely captured the movement's political horizons of the rebellion since the burning of the Third Precinct. The George Floyd Rebellion was set in motion by acts of actively obliterating police infrastructure and capacities: attacking precincts, setting cop cars afire, skirmishing with cops in the street, and laying bare the violent relationship at the heart of U.S. policing in scenes where, for once, both sides were fighting. By this point in the rebellion, however, the imperative to abolish had come to stand for a process of campaigning to convince politicians to shift funding away from police and toward social welfare programs, as part of a strategy to wear down the systems of policing and prisons on a protracted historical scale. Abolition thus had two meanings simultaneously: one which called for direct confrontation with police and their infrastructure, and another that sought to weaken the power of prisons and police through the mediation of electoral politics.

If the latter was the message meant to be conveyed by the graffiti on the Community Corrections building, however, it would not stand for long; a crowd had already breached the building and set it on fire. Within an hour it was a smoldering pile of rubble. The rhetorical exhortation to abolish had been superseded in real time by the practical abolition of the whole damn building.

The book you hold in your hand is the product of the same unique political moment that saw the Kenosha Community Corrections building meet its fiery demise. It is a moment of great flux, which singularly calls to mind the words of Marx and Engels that "all that is solid melts into air."[1] The COVID-19 pandemic has already proven to be the watershed sure to define the decades to come, in the same way 9/11 did for the first decades of the twenty-first century. Acute observers were quick to point out that the pandemic did not cause new social problems as much as it exacerbated and dramatized existing ones; COVID made the shocking poverty, racism, and deprivation at the heart of the "American Dream" a matter of undeniable urgency, rather than the stuff of a dull daily downward grind. The adaptability and indefinite staying power of the virus also provide a highly visible and disruptive biological analogue to the permanent crisis underlying social life. The explosion of the George Floyd Rebellion in the midst of the pandemic further heralded a new era in the bloody and violently contradictory history of the United States.

As we complete this book, the threatened political coup that dominated liberal imaginations for years has not come to pass—Donald Trump has surrendered the reins of power with the parting words "Have a good life," and liberals are celebrating a return to "normal" with the coming of the Biden presidency. But this is an impossible fantasy, even if it were a desirable one, which it is not. The present moment is akin to the interregnum period Antonio Gramsci wrote about, when "the old is dying and the new cannot be born," and "a great variety of morbid symptoms appear."[2]

By virtue of being born into this chaotic stage of world history, we have been condemned to try to understand it. This book is the product of a series of interrelated investigations into the interregnum period which saw the eruption of COVID, the

George Floyd Rebellion, and the spectacle of a resurgent radical right matched only in its militancy by an insurrectionary movement against the police. It is this last item which serves as our point of departure. In attempting to make sense of the George Floyd Rebellion, in which we were enthusiastic participants, we have returned time and again to the central objects of its attack: police stations, courthouses, correctional buildings, cop cars, and often the cops themselves. We have each spent considerable time, individually and collaboratively, exploring the history and concrete consequences of how carceral institutions have become enmeshed in the daily life of the racialized u.s. working class. In the wake of the Ferguson rebellion, we witnessed a dramatic uptick of interest around these topics, sufficient to find us both employed as university professors tasked with explaining the rise of the behemoth commonly referred to as "the carceral state." While our primary interest in these questions comes from experiences in social movements like Occupy Wall Street, the Ferguson rebellion and the months of frenzied street activity which solidified the original iteration of Black Lives Matter, and a variety of local campaigns between these great eruptions, it was clear in May 2020: we had never seen anything like the George Floyd Rebellion.

As the flames of Minneapolis still smoldered, liberals scrambled to recast the rebellion as *nonviolent civil disobedience*, the opening act for *dialogue* and *healing*, as part of *America's long overdue reckoning with systemic racism*, or else an urgent clarion cry for *police reform*. Ironically, the u.s. right, obsessively chronicling every window smashed, often provided more factual reporting on the militancy on the ground than the liberals, as illustrated by the widely mocked image of cnn reporter Omar Jimenez broadcasting from the flames of Kenosha atop the chyron: "Fiery but Mostly Peaceful Protest After Police Killing."

"They are trying to make the burning cop cars disappear, to extinguish from memory the police stations on fire, as if it didn't happen," writes Idris Robinson. "They're doing their best to make the event disappear."[3] At its core, the George Floyd Rebellion was no peaceful exercise in liberal-democratic citizenship serving as an overture for healing, which is a synonym for returning to normal. It was an outright attack on an entire way of life, characteristic of a capitalist order in violent decline. Rebels constituted a powerful negative force striking out against American society itself and the violent coercion that holds it all together. Based on our observation, study, participation, and subsequent hindsight, we now endeavor to present in as complete a form as possible the contours of this unique historical moment, where it came from, and where it could be headed.

Chapter One builds on writing from the first two weeks of the rebellion, originally published as "Prelude to a Hot American Summer."[4] At the time we predicted that the rebellion would reverberate throughout the summer, and this optimism was soon proven well founded. We drew from our past investigations into the development of the carceral state, the present arrangement of power by which police, prisons, courts, and nonprofit organizations linked to the punishment system have assumed a central role in u.s. social life. We were also attentive to another theme of our previous work, the idea that the constellation of police and prison infrastructure that bears the name "mass incarceration" is not static, but is in fact undergoing important shifts, sometimes even in tandem with seemingly liberal social actors, and is unafraid of adopting the language of social justice.[5]

Convinced that the targets of the rebellion were no accident, we attempted to situate the summer's events not just in relation to racism and police violence, which are surely important issues, but as a broader rejection of an entire way of life based on widespread human disposability, buttressed by a white-supremacist culture, and propped up, in the final instance, by the repressive organs of the state, chief among them the police. We recognized the George Floyd Rebellion as the opening salvo in a potentially large-scale repudiation of American capitalism, a manner of living in which inanimate objects are prized more highly than the majority of the human population. In this book, we have considerably revised and expanded our original article to incorporate subsequent reflection and new developments since its publication.

Chapter Two takes a step back, to situate the carceral state in historical and theoretical terms. Why is it that the United States, in the twenty-first century, keeps so many of its people in cages or other forms of compulsory restraint? Drawing on the Marxian tradition of prison studies, we emphasize the role of the punishment system in disciplining and regulating the working class. We also approach the question of how the application of this system has become so explicitly racialized in the United States. Against the vulgar binary of "race or class," we propose a dynamic conception of how the punishment system operates as a specifically racialized form of class domination, rooted in the capitalist imperative to repress, regulate, or dispose of the bottom tiers of the workforce in a period when many people are simply not needed by the market. This is the system of coercion and control, we argue, that the rebels who led the way in the George Floyd Rebellion took as their primary target. Similarly, this is the system that now seeks to incorporate the movement into its own perpetuation.

In Chapter Three, we examine how mass criminalization has become an experience shared by millions of working-class Americans, especially Black and Latinx ones. We argue that this is symptomatic of larger transformations in global capitalism in general, and of the American capitalist state in particular. In the face of a deepening capitalist crisis, revealing limits to the system's survival and ability to reproduce itself, policing, courts, and prisons have become indispensable tools of social control. While we pay close attention to the prison as an institution, we also examine the far reaches of the carceral state, including the most mundane encounters with the punishment system.

In the changing carceral landscape, several new practices have responded to the growing public dissatisfaction with the prison by presenting options which might not be brick-and-mortar sites of incarceration but continue to punish and stigmatize the poor nonetheless. We examine the transformations, on local and national levels, in how repressive state and local agencies—and, we will add, nonprofit organizations—manage the poverty and misery of the u.s. working class.

We further develop this theme in Chapter Four, where we examine the role that reforms have played in the development of the carceral state. As Michel Foucault famously observed, prison reformers and prisons were born at the same moment.[6] The history of incarceration in modernity is the history of reformers meeting crises of legitimacy with new plans for better methods of punishment. We see these forces active today when, amid a growing crisis of legitimacy surrounding mass incarceration, right-wing billionaires and "progressives" have found common ground in seeking to downsize the prison system while remaining fully committed to punishing the poor.

At the same time, a lucrative wing of the nonprofit sector that we dub "carceral nonprofits" has emerged to help develop diffuse state capacities for repression that shift the focus away from the prison and toward working-class communities at large.[7] Additionally, we explore the figure of police reform, which has long been a contentious issue for social movements, and became doubly so in the aftermath of the Ferguson rebellion. We argue that efforts to reform prisons and police function to rescue these institutions from crises of legitimacy, allowing them to shore up local support among petty bourgeois "community leaders," and generally steer the momentum and energy of activism and rebellion against the carceral state into bureaucratic channels. There, deprived of the oxygen that comes only from mass activity, they either perish or, worse yet, function to expand the carceral net.

We continue this thread in Chapter Five, in a discussion of a political tendency that has risen to prominence amid the George Floyd Rebellion, thanks to its sophisticated analysis of the carceral state, and program for its defeat: abolitionism. In making sense of the politics that captured the imagination of the George Floyd Rebellion, we explore the historical roots of abolitionism in both the movement against slavery in the United States, and more recently, the Black, Latinx, and Red Power movements of the 1960s and '70s, which established the basic political outlook still followed by many of today's abolitionists. We then turn a critical eye on the abolitionist conception of "non-reformist reforms," with special attention to how this practice has played out in recent campaigns to defund the police. This campaign harnessed the momentum of a movement that began with the setting of a police station alight and led it into a "slow build" quest for social change through policy initiatives offered in the same halls of power to which the rebellion laid siege. It is therefore deserving of particular scrutiny.

By way of a conclusion, we reflect on a change that is very much still underway. As of this writing, the United States is still partially "locked down." Despite alarmism in the left and right alike, the u.s. state has not gained new powers verging on total-itarianism; it can barely get people to accept the COVID vaccine. Instead, what we are seeing is a push to accept living with a deadly virus and continuous state disinvestment, where a large portion of the population can literally drop dead for all the government cares. As custodians of this racialized disinvestment, the police continue their daily business of brutality, befitting the violent order they enforce. The various bailout packages mounted by the federal government, born of austerity politics, and further adulterated by their filtering through the states, can only go so far to cushion the harshness of life in a society where perennial social crisis has become the status quo. The issue of eviction in particular—largely staved off by various state and federal measures—is emblematic of the way that u.s. politicians are only biding time. After all, the rent will eventually come due, and millions of Americans simply won't have it. Therefore, as we pause amid an unfolding catastrophe to gather some thoughts on its meaning and where it might be headed, we hope to have provided a basic set of propositions, or even just the questions that animate them, to a new generation of political actors emboldened by the rebellion and dissatisfied with the same old nostrums of slow and patient reform.

The George Floyd Rebellion, which offered tantalizing glimpses of a new world growing in the husk of the old, has only heightened both the promise and the pitfalls of political subjectivity in the most violent society the world has ever known. It is from the brave rebels taking action in America's streets that we have learned much of what we outline in this book. We are particularly grateful for the hard-won insights from a number of dedicated rebels across the country who took the time to speak with us, share their experiences, and provide feedback on our draft material. You know who you are. We offer what follows as a gift in return, and hope it can be of some use in the struggles ahead.

one

A Hot American Summer

The most dangerous creation of any society is the [person] who has nothing to lose.

JAMES BALDWIN[1]

In the unfolding of social antagonism that drives human history, there are spectacular moments when a hitherto invisible threshold is crossed and great masses who have long appeared to suffer in silence thrust themselves onto center stage to claim their place as breakers of chains and makers of history. The self-immolation of Tunisian street vendor Tarek el-Tayeb Mohamed Bouazizi in 2010 was one such event. The plan in 2016 to construct the Dakota Access oil pipeline across sacred indigenous land and water was another. In May 2020, the police murder of George Floyd, played and replayed millions of times around a world wracked by the COVID-19 pandemic, set alight a great wave of struggle the likes of which the United States had not seen in a half-century. Racist violence is not a new feature of American society; it is intrinsic to American capitalism, which is to say, intrinsic to the country itself. George Floyd was only among the latest in a pantheon of victims whose lives ended at the deadly nexus of racist exploitation and violence that holds the country together. So why George Floyd, and why 2020?

In a better world than ours, any death as callous and senseless as Floyd's murder would spark scenes of righteous indignation like those we saw in the summer of 2020. But in the contemporary United States, defined as it is by a banal daily spectacle of pointless, slow violence and wasted life—especially the lives of working-class Black people—the events set in motion by the murder of a regular working-class man on a nondescript American street require a closer look. In particular, the u.s. police, gatekeepers of the largest prison system on the planet, represent a particular form of capitalist social order managed by a state which prioritizes punishment and repressive social control to safeguard and reproduce itself. This is the carceral state. In 2020 we saw the widespread rejection of this order across the political spectrum, even predating Floyd's murder, exacerbated considerably by a pandemic that laid bare how little u.s. capitalism values most lives. By the time the video of Derek Chauvin's heinous act went viral, millions of ordinary people were ready to move. And their targeting of the police and other carceral infrastructure revealed the George Floyd Rebellion to be more than a quest for "justice" however defined, but the proactive and at times violent rejection of this entire way of life. "All institutions have lost legitimacy," writes the anarchist collective Inhabit: "the government, the cops, the media, the economy. The law has shown itself for what it is: sad, scared men draped in a Blue Lives Matter flag crying when the lights go out."[2]

In the months leading up to George Floyd's murder, the coronavirus brought much of the global economy to a halt, placing at least 36 million Americans on some type of unemployment relief, while demonstrating the shocking inadequacy of American public infrastructure to protect vulnerable people, especially Black people, from the physical and economic ravages of covid. "The old African-American aphorism 'When white America catches a cold, Black America gets pneumonia' has a new, morbid twist," writes Keeanga-Yamahtta Taylor: "when white

America catches the novel coronavirus, black Americans die."³ Surely Taylor would not dispute the staggering death toll among white America. But she correctly argues that African Americans were hit hardest by the pandemic because of longstanding structural inequalities and social determinants of health—dense and overcrowded housing, lack of access to healthy food and clean air, stress, trauma related to poverty and racism, and a tendency toward being employed in essential work in dense workplaces without adequate protections.⁴ Caught in the trap of structural racism in employment, housing, and health care, and a political system thoroughly rooted in appeals to white supremacy, ranging from the ordinary dog whistles to the airhorn sounded by Trump, Black Americans have been infected at three times the rate of white people and have been roughly twice as likely to die.⁵

But the disaster extended far beyond Black America. As COVID ravaged the world economy, many Americans who previously considered themselves secure, or even "middle-class," to use an oft-abused term, were confronted with the specter of interminable joblessness, a looming fear of evictions, a dire lack of hospital beds and health services, and the startling fragility of a world market on which we are all forced to depend for subsistence. Meanwhile, politicians and business elites openly debated the magnitude of human sacrifice necessary to getting the economy moving again, as vital aid packages were hung up by political theater. The two social actors most useless for the duration of the COVID pandemic, politicians and cops, received the vaccine before most Americans. In Chicago, Mayor Lori Lightfoot diverted $281.5 million of COVID relief into the payroll of the police.⁶ Even when a vaccine was introduced, these skewed priorities continued. "After eight long months of not wearing masks and spitting in the faces of protestors," tweeted journalist Jon Ben-Menachem, "NYPD cops get to line up early for vaccinations."

However, the macabre calculation on display in COVID relief negotiations in Washington, DC, is nothing new. For decades the

U.S. ruling class has shirked the brunt of sluggish profit rates, capital flight, and recurring economic crisis by stripping away the standard of living for working people, replacing the proverbial carrot of wealth redistribution with the stick of policing and incarceration. Even before the virus appeared on the scene, there were signs that the U.S. working class had been pushed too far. A national strike wave in education and nursing in the years before COVID hit demonstrated that many sectors are ready to fight back against a society where the central figure of social reproduction is the policeman's club. Similarly, years of upheaval behind bars in U.S. prisons indicate that the largest national prison population in the world actively contests this regime, even from within some of the most repressive environments imaginable.

Running Out of Patience

> I'm sick and tired of being sick and tired.
>
> FANNIE LOU HAMMER[7]

The central narrative figure of the rebellion became the enduring color line in U.S. society. The racial hierarchy that has ordered American society since its colonial period became an object of scrutiny on an unprecedented scale. George Floyd's life and death speak to the visceral double system of justice that operates in the United States, part and parcel of a system in which life is cheap, Black life most of all. According to recent analysis from Harvard University School of Public Health, Black people are 3.3 times more likely to be killed by police than are white people.[8] As the authors of the study argue, these racial disparities in police killings vary greatly across the United States and are more striking in metropolitan areas. For example, they found that Black Chicagoans are 650 times more likely to be killed by police than their white counterparts.[9] In Minneapolis, at least since 2000, 25 percent of all police killings in Minneapolis have been African

Americans, while they comprise 19 percent of the city's overall population. The list of names and occupations of those killed by the Minneapolis Police includes mostly working-class people: day laborers, truck drivers, mechanics, salesclerks, security guards, students, and the unemployed.[10] It is important to note that the combination of the postwar reconfiguration of cities, including decades of deindustrialization; racial discrimination in housing and employment; and the transformations in modern policing has concentrated police power specifically on racially segregated Black neighborhoods.[11] Data shows that in Minnesota, high-poverty areas have a 3.5 times higher percentage of police killings than wealthier areas; Black and Latinx people tend to live more often in higher poverty areas than white people.[12]

This disparity in police violence reflects disparities in wealth. On the surface, Floyd's home city of Minneapolis seemed to have weathered the devastating effects of deindustrialization better than similarly sized cities such as St. Louis. Minneapolis and St. Paul, the Twin Cities, have been dubbed "the Midwestern Miracle," with nineteen Fortune 500 companies calling the area their home. In 2018, the Twin Cities ranked twentieth among the 25 richest cities in America. Yet this prosperity has been mostly concentrated at the top, completely leaving out its Black residents, making it two cities in more ways than one.[13] Samuel L. Myers Jr., an economist at the University of Minnesota, coined the term the "Minnesota Paradox" to make sense of this phenomenon.[14] Minnesota's racial wealth gap is third in the country after District of Colombia and Wisconsin.[15] While well-off white residents enjoy standards of living comparable with those of other high-income cities, working-class Black residents navigate underfunded schools, racial segregation in housing and employment, and high rates of joblessness—all of which are reinforced by the punishment system. The median Black family in the Twin Cities earns half of what its white counterpart makes.[16] In 2016, the year that Philando Castile was killed by a policeman in a neighborhood just 15 minutes away from the center of the George Floyd protests, Black Minnesotans were three times more likely than white Minnesotans to be unemployed.[17]

These racial inequalities are even more starkly represented in the justice system: in 2019, Black residents were eleven times more likely than white residents to experience incarceration.[18] One of the major ways that Black Minnesotans come into contact with the carceral state is through street-level policing. In a report concerning arrest data between January 2012 and September 2014, the American Civil Liberties Union (ACLU) found that the Minneapolis Police Department made "almost 100 low-level arrests per day." Black residents were 8.7 times more likely than white residents to be arrested for low-level offenses; Native Americans were 8.6 more likely. According to the study, Black Minnesotans make up only 19 percent of the city population but account for 59 percent of low-level arrests, concentrated in the predominantly Black neighborhoods in North and South Minneapolis that surround the city's downtown center.[19] The George Floyd Rebellion exposed this dark side of the Twin Cities' prosperity, well known to residents, for the rest of America to see.

As Democrats and nonprofit organizations quickly called for "reform" of the police amid the George Floyd Rebellion, the recent history of Minneapolis itself in fact provides us with front-row seats to the tragicomedy that this entails. In their review of the Minneapolis Police Department's misconduct over the past five decades, the abolitionist collective MPD150 have argued that these cycles of police reform have done nothing to challenge police violence and instead have only worked to "temporarily pacify resistance from victimized communities without altering police business as usual."[20] The last decade and a half of police reform is instructive. In 2007, five Black police officers sued the Minneapolis Police Department for racial discrimination, and accused Bob Kroll, a sergeant and president of the Police Officers

Federation of Minneapolis, of making racist and homophobic remarks, and even sporting a motorcycle jacket bearing the motto "white power."[21] Two years later, an investigation into the Metro Gang Strike Force, a multi-agency collaboration between the Minneapolis Police Department and other state agencies to supposedly combat gang violence, found widespread misconduct among its employees and officers, including illegal searches and seizures, and cops simply taking property from people who were not suspects.[22]

When veteran police officer Janeé Harteau was appointed in 2012 as the city's first female and openly gay police chief, she vowed to overhaul the force and embraced change along lines advocated by the Obama administration.[23] In 2015, in the aftermath of the Ferguson rebellion, Minneapolis was selected by the Department of Justice as one of six cities to undergo reform efforts as part of Obama's national My Brother's Keeper initiative. In three years, $4.75 million was spent to collect data and come up with a list of evidence-based practices to repair community-police relations. The result was Harteau's MPD 20: *A New Police Model*, aimed at shifting the Minneapolis Police Department (MPD) to so-called community policing. According to MPD 150, this initiative was nothing more than a public relations move.[24] If that was the case, it worked. Before MPD became known for the killing of George Floyd, it had become something of a national poster child for police reform.

Community policing is a famously vacuous concept, meaning just about anything a cop does after getting out of their car. But, however toothless, Harteau's initiative was widely resisted by rank-and-file police officers. Two years later, a damning report by the Department of Justice accused the MDP of failing to discipline officers charged with misconduct. The MPD found loopholes to avoid police suspensions and other forms of discipline and instead sent its officers to "coaching sessions," which amounted to reading the police manual out loud.[25] In 2016, the MPD rewrote its policy regarding the use of force and instituted new rules that required police officers to intervene in moments where fellow officers were being abusive. Other changes were introduced, including training on procedural justice, implicit bias, and crisis intervention. Yet these changes were never embraced by the rank and file. A year later, in the wake of the MPD murder of forty-year-old Australian American Justine Damond, Chief Harteau quit her post. In 2018, the MPD received plaudits in police reform circles for supposedly leading the nation in terms of embracing procedural change—despite still more public outrage over a police killing, this time of a 31-year-old Black man named Thurman Blevins.[26] Since 2000, law enforcement officers in Minnesota have killed 215 people, most of them working-class, and disproportionately Black.[27] This is where the rebellion began; is it any wonder?

Growing up under the shadow of 9/11, it seemed almost a miracle to behold the cult of cop worship coming undone before our very eyes. The contrast between the Ferguson rebellion and the previous iteration of Black Lives Matter (BLM) is stark, perhaps especially considering the fact that criminally charging the killer cops, which was a primary demand of the 2014 movement, did not appease rebels in 2020. But we can go further back. Every anti-police riot in American history, from at least 1919 to the present, has ended with an acknowledgment of the material deficits of resources and social power shaping police violence against Black Americans and an arrival at two main solutions: police reform and the promise of job opportunities for Black youth. Today, it seems, such crumbs are not enough. After decades of attempts to tinker with the institution of policing, it is becoming impossible to ignore that no amount of police reform seems capable of stopping cops from killing Black people. Making police forces and their civilian bosses more "diverse" has similarly proven to be a dead end. Reflecting on the Baltimore riots of 2015, Keeanga-Yamahtta Taylor writes: "When a Black mayor, governing a largely Black city, aids in the mobilization of a military unit led by a Black woman to suppress a Black rebellion, we are in a new period of the Black freedom struggle."[28]

It would be impossible to outline singular motives for the upward of 26 million people who took part in the rebellion.[29] We can, however, understand the rebellion as the grasping for a collective response to crisis in a society where people are socialized to struggle alone and crave above all personal autonomy, with individualized survival techniques such as petty shoplifting more emblematic of America's response to crises than the much heralded but evasive rent strikes.[30] Alongside the fear of impending death which COVID wrought lurked the prospect of a life of poverty, as Americans watched their livelihoods crumble, bills amass unpaid, and mortgages and rents come due and past due. Is it any wonder that the horrific sight of a man being slowly choked to death while pleading for his life has found such widespread resonance?

What is most distinctive about the rebellion is not that Americans acted out of desperation, which is a consistent feature of life for most Americans, but that they did it cooperatively. A critical mass of Americans got sick of hating their society as private individuals and decided to despise it openly and in concert. It was at once the rejection of an entire world and a concrete step toward building a new one. The order rejected by the George Floyd Rebellion is the carceral state, an amalgamation of police, jails, and prisons tasked with keeping the violent contradictions of society under control. By the carceral state, we mean an interconnected network of punishment institutions inside and outside of prisons, including the variety of coercive institutions often represented as "alternatives to incarceration," such as probation, parole, mandatory drug treatment, house arrest, and other related institutions.[31] This definition, which draws from a long tradition of U.S. prison industrial complex (PIC) abolitionists, enables us to explode the false binary between this network and incarceration itself. The concept of the carceral state allows us to understand more deeply the nature of the state in the lives of the poor and to be critical of institutions that extend far beyond the usual suspects such as policing and prisons. Today, repressive social control and punishment have penetrated all state governing institutions beyond simply those that police incarnate and control: schools, perfunctory work for welfare recipients, social workers often indistinguishable from probation officers who are themselves often indistinguishable from prison guards and cops.

"The NYPD infiltrated everyday life more and more as they gradually absorbed government functions that had nothing to do with policing," writes the anonymous author of "The Only Way Out Is Always Through the Police."

> Police were now feeding the poor, doing homeless outreach, opening playgrounds, running after school STEM [science, technology, engineering, and mathematics] education programs, conducting Narcan training, teaching financial literacy, running résumé-writing workshops, hosting church breakfasts, collecting e-waste, fixing flats, microchipping pets, mentoring at-risk youth. New "neighborhood policing" initiatives turned cops into social workers with guns, guidance counselors with guns, janitors with guns, preachers with guns. Cops weren't cops, they were community advocates empowered to use violence to keep neighborhoods quiet, calm, and orderly.[32]

In matters of policing and austerity, it is often the case that as goes New York, so goes the nation. In the pustulant oozing of the cops into every crevice of working-class life, New York may stand out in terms of its funding and the militancy of its cops, but it is largely part of a national picture by which the cops have remade society in their own image and seized control of key social institutions.

Following Ruth Wilson Gilmore, Tony Platt, Christian Parenti, and others, we also understand the carceral state as the result of a concrete historical shift in the allocation of public funds, state capacity, and really the entire collective imagination of much of u.s. society amid decades of social instability wrought by capitalist crisis.[33] The 2008 crisis was a symptom of the structural difficulties that the u.s. and other advanced countries entered after a postwar boom, when the state, buoyed by the profits of industrial capital at home and imperialism abroad, took greater responsibility for providing services and building infrastructure. By the 1960s, however, capitalism's stagnant growth amid overproduction, and the ruling class's unwillingness to foot the bill for "welfare state" expenditure, put tremendous pressure on state and city budgets, as capital became more global and capitalists became untethered from any national or even local obligations. Cities like New York, for instance, responded by cutting back and privatizing social services and initiating austerity policies that placed the onus on working-class New Yorkers to do more with less.

New York City's 1974 fiscal crisis was a microcosm of the wider national crisis, the ruling class reply to which found expression in President's Ford's response to requests for a federal bailout, which the *Daily News* tersely summarized as: "drop dead." Far from a bailout of the so-called welfare state, the fiscal crisis occasioned the ascendancy of the finance, insurance, and real estate (FIRE) sector as the dominant force in u.s. politics, at a time when capitalists were increasingly frustrated in low- or no-profit industrial pursuits and sought new productive outlets in financialization and real-estate speculation across the globe. While industrial capital requires a relatively healthy stock of workers, the FIRE sector cares not for even the most basic quality of life for the vast majority of working-class Americans, and has thus undertaken the wholesale gutting of what was only ever a meager welfare state apparatus. This shift was accompanied by the rise of an ideologically racist political current under the banner of "law and order" that combined urban crisis, urban rebellion, and political radicalism into a racialized threat to be defeated by a strong security state and the defense of traditional white power. The culmination of this movement was the election of Donald Trump, who differed from his Republican predecessors on issues of race and crime mostly just by virtue of saying things out loud.

In place of public expenditures taken directly from state funds, nonprofit organizations have arisen which can cushion the blows raining down on the racialized working class in a way conducive to capitalist development, cultivating local petty-bourgeois actors and sowing pro-business attitudes while simultaneously controlling the purse strings of public assistance in ways that the public sector cannot. This new configuration has the dual advantage of serving as a cheaper way to reproduce workers—especially those made redundant by deindustrialization—while simultaneously repressing the political will of working-class people by crushing the idea that society owes them anything at all. Despite isolated struggles that are the exception that proves the rule, the u.s. since the 1970s has seen, in communist theorist Loren Goldner's words, "a class war in which only one side was fighting."[34] But the George Floyd Rebellion demonstrated that this social order may not hold for much longer. "When history is written as it ought to be written," wrote C.L.R. James, "it is the moderation and long patience of the masses at which [people] will wonder, not their ferocity."[35]

Get in the Zone

> Shoutout to my friends at home on the couch! I did it! I'm here! I'm the man!
> Protester outside the burning Third Precinct, May 28, 2020[36]

In the early days of the George Floyd Rebellion, one thing certain was that American cities were no longer ghost towns. "COVID is over!" declared a shirtless-yet-masked protester, pumping his fist amid the flames of Minneapolis. In the days following Floyd's murder, the now-infamous Third Precinct, home to Derek Chauvin and his accomplices, was set afire alongside an AutoZone, a Target, a liquor store, other local businesses, and a condominium under construction. For a time, the Minneapolis police were nowhere to be found. Afraid and outnumbered, they awaited relief from the National Guard. Meanwhile, across the country, millions of people marched on previously deserted boulevards and highways, weaving along and crisscrossing the overpoliced streets of New York, Chicago, DC, and Philadelphia, but also along the Main Streets of smaller cities and towns. Three days after George Floyd's killers were charged, the streets of Washington, DC, erupted in flames. The headquarters of the American Federation of Labor and Congress of Industrial Organizations (AFL-CIO), a defender of the police unions in its ranks, was smashed and defaced. The rebellion even reached the gates of the White House. As protestors clashed with police, set the guardhouse on fire, and briefly breached the exterior fence, officials turned off the exterior lighting and President Trump hurried off to hide in a bunker. That same day, the National Guard was called in to Washington, DC, Georgia, Kentucky, Wisconsin, Colorado, Ohio, Tennessee, and Utah.

A new political moment was underway, defined by the rejection of the old world. "After the revolutionary movements all over the world in 2019," an anonymous Minneapolis rebel remarked, "I was afraid that the pandemic would throw us into a new dark era. But just when we all lost hope, America showed the world that nothing is over."[37]

While the name George Floyd has become synonymous with these events, the rebellion animated struggles around several tragic killings, such as those of Elijah McClain in Aurora, Colorado; Ahmaud Arbery in Brunswick, Georgia; and Breonna Taylor in Louisville, Kentucky. In its course, the police shooting

of Rayshard Brooks in Atlanta, Georgia, and Jacob Blake in
Kenosha, Wisconsin, triggered redoubled struggle in these cities
that resonated nationally. And these cases were only two of the
latest and most high-profile in a seemingly endless cascade of
white supremacist terror reminiscent of the *old* Jim Crow. Floyd's
case also recalls the stories of Eric Garner, Michael Brown, and
Sandra Bland, who perished at the hands of the carceral state after
trifling encounters, catalyzing in their wake the first incarnation
of BLM. These cases resonated with Black people who routinely
suffer these same indignities but without the lethal conclusion. "Martyrs drive this movement," wrote Tobi Haslett in
a passionate reflection on the George Floyd Rebellion:

> they are its origin and blazing emblems. But some of the most
> infamous police murders extend from more quotidian debase-
> ments . . . Eric Garner was harassed repeatedly before his
> death in 2014; police even took his exhausted fury at this as
> pretext to throw him to the ground. "I told you the last time,"
> he begs in the video recording as officers close in, "please
> leave me alone!"[38]

It is difficult to discuss the rebellion as a singular occur-
rence at all. One of the rebellion's many staggering features was
the extension of protests into small towns across the U.S. While
cities with long histories of struggle such as Portland and Seattle
attracted the lion's share of national press, there were more than
11,000 protests in over 3,000 different places throughout the
U.S., including all fifty states.[39] This massive dispersion of actions
ranged from peaceful rallies to outright insurrectionary gestures
like the siege of the Third Precinct. Simultaneously, the resur-
gence of the BLM movement further complicates matters; it is
at once a meme, a social movement, a tangled nexus of formal
organizations, and an abstract signifier that guided autonomous
organizing across the U.S. Anyone who speaks of BLM as a

singularity has probably never been to a protest. BLM is therefore an inadequate yet necessary signifier for the side of the rebellion which advocated traditional social movement protocol, such as orderly nonviolent protests, speaking truth to power, and working with local political and nonprofit machines. Alongside these more orthodox leftist groupings, a critical mass of people took direct action, battling police, attacking carceral infrastructure, and expropriating commodities. We do not support a line of demarcation between these two camps; in fact, the distinction between "good protester" and "bad protester" is a tool of the state, meant to defeat both. It remains one of the most remarkable features of the rebellion that it resisted this distinction as valiantly as it did. Therefore, we speak of the rebellion as a singular event without denying that it was an unstable and contradictory compound.[40]

The rebellion also resonated internationally, across an entire planet wracked by COVID and many of the same austerity policies which make life so cheap in the United States. In Greece, demonstrators hurled firebombs at the U.S. embassy in Athens in solidarity with those protesting Floyd's murder. Clashes with police also marked anti-police actions in Mexico and in England; a statue of a prominent slave trader was torn down and consigned to Bristol harbor, formerly a key node in the Atlantic slave trade. In Brazil, protesters held up signs that read "Our Brother George Floyd" as they clashed with riot-gear-clad police and demanded an end to the racist policing practices of the favelas by the Bolsonaro government. These were part of at least 8,700 demonstrations in 74 countries, bridging BLM solidarity with local struggles around police violence and racism.[41] As anti-police protests kicked off in Colombia, Nigeria, and elsewhere, it became a distinct possibility that future accounts of this rebellion could describe it as the beginning of a global offensive against the social order police violently uphold.

The rebellion was not uncontested, and its violent enemies were not just police. Small towns such as Bethel, Ohio, became the scenes of contentious standoffs between ad hoc BLM demonstrations and significant armed counter-protests organized by pro-police thugs, fueled in part by online rumors of impending droves of out of town "Antifa and BLM" rioters. The violence visited on Bethel antiracists by vigilantes was an early indication of the violence to come by self-styled civilian defenders of "law and order" willing to repress the rebellion by force. The narrative of bat-wielding white goon squads in Philadelphia's Fishtown and Chicago's Bridgeport—defending against a threat which never materialized—was perhaps the more common story, but many armed right-wingers menaced actually existing demonstrations and committed great violence. These vigilantes had significant overlap with armed protests against public health measures and COVID safety regulations commonly called "the lockdown." In response to the devastation that market dependence has visited on U.S. households, they do not blame capitalism, but America's insufficient appetite for human sacrifice to keep the market roaring. And this milieu, which produced Kenosha shooter Kyle Rittenhouse, bridges pro-Trump and pro-police activists, right-wing militias like the Oath Keepers and Three-Percenters, followers of QAnon and Infowars, remnants of the alt-right such as the neofascist street gang Proud Boys, and cops themselves, who are counted among donors to Rittenhouse's legal defense. In fact, by October, the number of demonstrations for right-wing causes had surpassed that of left-wing causes, including BLM.[42]

In the key months of 2020, however, the momentum belonged to the rebellion. Its large unpermitted marches and infrastructure blockades called to mind the BLM movement at its post-Ferguson peak. In big cities, groups of demonstrators at once jubilant and enraged moved through streets made impassable to auto traffic, scattering into meandering snake marches, reconverging by accident amid cheers of joy. These street scenes furnished an organic anarchic environment for a wide range of tactics, whether they be anti-cop graffiti, expropriation of goods, pitched battles with the police, or simply feeling the collective power of shutting down the streets without begging the city for permission first.

COVID mutual aid networks were repurposed to provide food, water, and masks to sustain protesters throughout the course of long marches, while these practices were also taken up by individual people announcing their free wares with signs on their backpacks or cars. In Chicago, cars parked along march routes, distributing hand sanitizer through the driver's side window. Car caravans also provided a safer way for people vulnerable to COVID to participate—and snarl traffic in the process, often with passengers protruding through sunroofs, waving signs, and dancing. They also made roads impassable for police seeking to use violence against rebels. Cars, a fixture of American culture for better or worse, also served to furnish a particular collective and cooperative form of expropriation, such as in the looting caravan that laid siege to Chicago's posh Magnificent Mile shopping district.[43] At a time when mutual aid has become another word for charity, such acts could be seen to represent a more direct form of mutual aid that points to a bridge between simply reproducing class relations by enabling a base line of survival, and going on the offensive against the regime of private property that makes survival so precarious in the first place.

A word is in order here about expropriation itself or, as it is commonly called, looting. At its root, the rebellion was a direct attack on carceral infrastructure and a vociferous rejection of the social order of the carceral state. While many people prefer to remember otherwise, in the political climate of 2020, attacks on cops and their shiny toys were actually quite popular. But a secondary, and more controversial, figure, was that of looting. "Once it is no longer bought," wrote the Situationist International in the wake of the Watts Rebellion, "the commodity lies open to criticism and alteration, whatever particular form it may take. Only when it is paid for with money is it respected as an admirable fetish, as a symbol of status within the world of survival."[44] By contrast, there is a tendency to dismiss looting outright as anti-social and devoid of meaning. In the wake of the riots in England in 2011, contrarian public intellectual Slavoj Žižek argued that the rioters could not be conceived as revolutionists in a Marxist sense, and "fit much better the Hegelian notion of the 'rabble', those outside organized social space, who can express their discontent only through 'irrational' outbursts of destructive violence—what Hegel called 'abstract negativity'."[45] These two approaches are dialectical opposites, as Hegel himself would say. They assume that looting means the same thing in all the contexts it is deployed in, and is either a pure expression of revolutionary agency, or nothing at all. At bottom, this is just philosophical dress on an old-fashioned binary of good/bad.

We argue instead that looting must be understood as instrumental, part of its unique political contexts.[46] The act of looting itself has no intrinsic value. In the George Floyd Rebellion, looting represented above all a moment of freedom from the carceral state, premised on the rejection of the legitimacy of the entire social order, in which the content of liberation was creatively explored. "No activity more directly confirms the absence of police control over a territory, the suspension and inoperativity of the law, than looting," writes Adrian Wohlleben.[47] Looting can have any number of purposes—stealing to survive, stealing for fun, stealing to prey on other proletarians by selling for a profit, stealing to keep a riot or siege of a police precinct going. It can have all of these at once. The anonymous author of "Siege of the Third Precinct in Minneapolis" argues that looting served three critical aims:

> First, it liberated supplies to heal and nourish the crowd . . .
> Second, looting boosted the crowd's morale by creating solidarity and joy through a shared act of collective transgression . . . Third, and most importantly, looting contributed to keeping the situation ungovernable. As looting spread throughout the city, police forces everywhere were spread thin.[48]

This allowed for the precinct to be taken down. Looting was therefore an experiment in freedom from the meshes of the carceral state, preliminary steps toward understanding what it could mean to be free of the domination of the cops and the capitalist order that they prop up. Much like the attacks on carceral infrastructure, which signal a rejection of a particular world order and demand the positive content of building the world that should take its place, looting heralds the beginning of politics—not a politics in and of itself.

The massive crowds where these militant tactics blended with more traditional left rituals were remarkable not just in scope, but ferocity. Demonstrations across the u.s. saw police cars set on fire, businesses targeted, and goods expropriated in cities big and small. In response to police violence, protesters tossed bottles, bricks, and Molotov cocktails, returned volleys of tear gas cans, and shot fireworks. Following the examples of Hong Kong and Santiago, Chile, in 2019, some used lasers to impair cops' vision, immobilize surveillance drones, and force police helicopters to retreat. Umbrellas proved a remarkably versatile tool, protecting against pepper spray and shattered glass, blunting the impact of rubber bullets, and providing cover from the photographers who descended like vultures on riots with no concern for the consequences of documenting illegal activity. The explicit adoption of this "front-liner" culture, of which the umbrella is the symbol, represented not just an ensemble of riot tools, or a mode of dress, but a philosophy of how small groups of dedicated militants can successfully deepen a rebellion in progress. "The basic idea," writes the collective Chuang,

> allowing the concept of the frontline to integrate the movement beyond the old divides between violence and nonviolence, or "diversity tactics," is that those on the frontlines take personal risks to protect those around them, ideally with (but often without) distinctive protective

gear, and that these risks help to push forward the entire movement.[49]

It was remarkable how quickly this sensibility generalized across the u.s., albeit in small blocs within the movement.

The essay "The Siege of the Third Precinct in Minneapolis," which offers a painstaking account of how the battle went down, is indispensable for understanding this tactical gamut. It explores in detail how the adoption of front-liner culture provided a de facto field manual for a hard core of militants in the successful capture of that building. Most interesting about this text is its rejection of the division between nonviolence and violence. The author argues instead that there was an important role for actions that could be grouped into both, admittedly fraught, categories. Even the "hands up, don't shoot" tactic pioneered in the streets of Ferguson, often misunderstood as a symbol of pacifism, was a confrontational tactic when facing down a police line, while also allowing those pursuing more militant tactics necessary cover.[50]

Similarly, a variety of political issues provided an umbrella for militant direct action, perhaps especially through the practice of attacking statues. Statues honoring paragons of white supremacy were targeted across the u.s.; it was open season on all symbols of an entire social order. At least 38 statues were seriously damaged or outright toppled by brave and resourceful crowds who gave up on petitions and speaking truth to power and decided to take the damned things down themselves.[51] While this type of politics risks fixating on representation—changing a city's statues does not alter its racial order—this issue provided the basis for building communal bonds based on shared illegality and risk-taking. In Chicago, a coordinated operation undertaken by demonstrators in black-bloc formation repelled police with fireworks and projectiles, laying siege to a Christopher Columbus statue in broad daylight and using the appropriate force against any cop who stood in their way.

With the tight regulation of urban spaces shattered as if a spell had been lifted, scenes unfolded in iconic settings one would scarcely believe if they saw it on the big screen. "Outside the Strand Bookstore," writes the collective New York Post-Left:

> flaming barricades and volleys of bricks and bottles held back a small detachment of riot cops while hundreds danced in the street and shared looted bottles of whiskey. With the police spread thin by stand-offs, a crowd of mostly Black youth, organized in crews and dressed in black began quietly making their way downtown. Over the course of that night, the luxury stores of Soho were systematically looted. The cycle of rioting, dispersing, and reconvening until early in the morning.[52]

In New York City, 47 police vehicles were damaged in early June alone, at least thirteen of them torched by protestors. By late July, that number had increased to 303, a value of $1 million. In Chicago, roughly a hundred police cars were taken out of service, and anecdotes have been told of cop cars on patrol with broken windows and graffitied with anti-police slogans.[53] In Atlanta, protestors climbed the sign in front of CNN headquarters, spray-painted anti-police messages, and waved the Mexican flag. Philadelphians undertook numerous "ATM bombings"—literally the detonation of small explosives to expropriate the cash inside. Police departments and courthouse buildings were targeted by protestors in Nashville, Dallas, Denver, Phoenix, Las Vegas, and Portland. In Denver, protestors smashed the windows of the Colorado Judicial Center. They set off fireworks outside the federal buildings in downtown Las Vegas and damaged the federal courthouse. In Kenosha, as described in the introduction, a crowd burned down a Community Corrections building, where untold hours of peoples' lives had been wasted by the absurd and pointless rituals of probation. In Portland, protestors smashed windows and set fires inside the Multnomah County Justice Center while correctional staff manned the first floor. A similar attack followed in Oakland, where the Alameda County Courthouse was pelted and briefly set afire.

These two last sites, emblematic of the zeitgeist of open attack on infrastructure of the carceral state, would become a key flashpoint of struggle in the weeks and months that followed. Scenes of great heroism by Portland rebels played out against increasingly militarized police tactics. These nightly standoffs were exacerbated when President Trump dispatched what was in effect his own personal federal police force, comprised of loyalists from the Department of Homeland Security (DHS) and Customs and Border Patrol, against the wishes of Portland and Oregon governments. These agents appeared as an occupying army, wearing no identification, carrying automatic weapons with live ammunition, and abducting protesters in unmarked vans for extra-judicial interrogation.[54] The brutality of local and federal police prompted ingenious strategic innovations on the part of the rebels, including elaborate body armor, coordinated tactics like shield walls, the offensive deployment of fireworks, and creative re-appropriations of a variety of cheap commodities, like the use of leaf blowers to repel tear gas.[55] "Hand signals I had learned in the Army," remarked the pseudonymous Misanthrophile, were "discovered again by an army of Gen-Z warriors: stop, regroup, left, right, quiet down."[56] The figure of the government-trained soldier turned rebel, a source of ruling-class anxiety since at least the Vietnam War, and seen in cultural figures ranging from John Rambo to Killmonger in the recent *Black Panther* film, became a reality on streets across the u.s. And how could it not, with nearly two decades of uninterrupted imperialist wars churning out working-class malcontents?

The courage and determination of rebels was met with considerable police and vigilante violence, coast to coast. The forces of repression in Portland released so much tear gas into the air that the Oregon Department of Environmental Quality raised concerns that it could be polluting the Willamette river. In some cases, repression galvanized the movement. "What did the police state expect," reflects Misanthrophile, "when they trained us every night to withstand them?" The author concludes that "police made the mistake all authoritarians and cowards make: because they are driven by fear, they believe others are too."[57] But it is impossible to say that police violence against the rebellion did not have a chilling effect on participation. This is surely true of the tens of thousands of petty arrests, designed simply to demobilize and terrorize movement participants through often-violent arrests and lengthy periods of detainment, with charges frequently dropped later, since conviction of a criminal offense was never the point.

In the early weeks of the rebellion, hundreds of protesters were injured by police tear gas and rubber bullets. While rubber bullets are designed to be ricocheted off the ground, cops mostly fired them directly, often at point-blank range. In San Jose, rubber bullets maimed a local activist who worked to educate cops about their "implicit biases." One team of researchers found more than a hundred head injuries from rubber pullets in the first two months alone.[58] Similarly, while chemical agents are prohibited in foreign wars by the Geneva Convention, American police deployed them domestically, not only in Portland, but just about everywhere. In Louisville, Kentucky, the National Guard shot and killed David McAtee, the owner of a barbeque restaurant known for giving cops free meals. The cops also inflicted considerable violence and intimidation against reporters, including at least sixty arrests of journalists.

Perhaps the most dramatic act of direct repression was the extra-judicial execution of anti-fascist activist Michael Reinoehl, who was hunted down and summarily shot at the urging of President Trump. Reinoehl's offense was shooting—defensively, he asserted—a member of the armed proto-fascist group Patriot Prayer, which has been attacking leftists in the area for years.

"We sent in the U.S. Marshals," Trump bragged to a crowd at one of his subsequent rallies. "Took fifteen minutes, it was over . . . We got him. They knew who he was. They didn't want to arrest him, and [in] fifteen minutes, that ended."[59] Amid the years-long whiplash of Trump's latest affront to liberal democracy, this shocking admission of the extra-judicial execution of an American antifascist carried out at the orders of the president barely registered a blip in the national press. Surely the conspiracy theories about "outside agitators" and other malicious disinformation spread by enemies of the rebellion didn't help.

The rebellion also had a strong presence behind bars. According to an in-depth study by the publication *Perilous*, there were at least 119 instances of prisoner resistance in the U.S. and Canada in a ninety-day period beginning March 17, 2020, a dramatic rise in recorded instances of rebellion. Of these recorded incidents, seventeen included more than a hundred participants. The original context for this wave of resistance was the COVID crisis, which by November had claimed 1,412 prisoner lives and infected more than 182,000 incarcerated people in the U.S. and Canada alone. Early prisoner demands included basic precautionary measures, including personal protective equipment (PPE) and keeping sick prisoners out of the general population. In June, detainees at an Immigration and Customs Enforcement (ICE) facility in Arizona announced a hunger strike, their second of the year, with the proclamation:

> We, the detained people of dormitories A, B, and C at Mesa Verde ICE Detention Facility, are protesting and on hunger strike in solidarity with the detained people at Otay Mesa Detention Center. We begin our protest in memory of our comrades George Floyd, Breonna Taylor, Oscar Grant, and Tony McDade. Almost all of us have also suffered through our country's corrupt and racist punishment system before being pushed into the hands of ICE.[60]

Struggle in Atlanta around the June 12 killing of Rayshard Brooks continued after the alleged perpetrator was charged. In 2014, a key demand of the Black Lives Matter protests was to legally charge killer cops, but by 2020 that was too little, too late. Almost immediately, the charred Wendy's restaurant where Brooks was killed became a sort of open-air convergence point for the local rebellion. The Atlanta site was part of a broader national experiment, harking back to Occupy Wall Street, of creating open-air "autonomous zones," most famously CHOP/CHAZ in Seattle, and attempting to sustain them over time as a means of enhancing the rebellion, or as ends in themselves. But echoing a problem that dogged the movement in the waning days of summer, the focus of the Wendy's occupation became increasingly defined by arming for self-defense, and even widespread sentiments of laying down one's life for the struggle, though no clear revolutionary path lay ahead. This was due in no small part to the targeting of the occupation by armed white supremacists. The juxtaposition, however, of such high levels of tactical militancy with no clear strategic goal, deftly underscored by an anonymous account, "At the Wendy's: Armed Struggle at the End of the World," illustrated a broader feature of the rebellion, one that the collective Endnotes calls the "production of revolutionaries without a revolution."[61]

In NYC, a video showing Dominican men defending stores against alleged Black looters went viral and sparked important discussions and solidarity protests among Black and Latinx New Yorkers. In Chicago, Mexican organizers sponsored a solidarity rally attempting to bring together Black and Mexican youth, after considerable tension and anti-Black violence had occurred in the latter's communities in the heat of the rebellion. As can be expected in moments of great upheaval, just about everyone behaved as an exaggerated version of themselves, with all the contradictions inherent in the U.S. social order emerging in a chaotic eruption of antagonism and disharmony, even amid moments of

great popular solidarity. This confusion wrought by the chaos of
the rebellion provided an opening for its enemies.

Don't Believe the Hype

> These people who judge us should take a city bus or a cab through
> the South Bronx, the Central Ward of Newark, North Philadelphia,
> the Northwest section of the District of Columbia or any Third
> World reservation, and see if they can note a robbery in progress.
>
> KUWASI BALAGOON[62]

Aided by their mouthpieces in the press, from the earliest days of
the rebellion state officials did everything in their power to divide
the rebellion between "peaceful protesters" and "rioters"—the
latter portrayed as looters and opportunistic riffraff out to destroy
the social fabric of communities. In this lexicon, many tactics
in which no human body is harmed are classed as "violent,"
including the destruction of inanimate objects, the expropriation
of commodities for their use, and self-defense against police, who
were initiating violent encounters all over the country. Befitting a
society which privileges the value of private property over that of
human life, so-called looting proved to be a particularly divisive
issue. Interestingly, however, debates around expropriations,
as with those around arson, were focused almost solely on the
targeting of small businesses, with a noticeable lack of sympathy
for chain stores like Target and Wal-Mart.

"I grew up around these buildings," a protester in
Minneapolis proclaimed as the blocks around the Third Precinct
went up in flames. "Fuck these buildings. I used to get tacos here.
Fuck them tacos. Fuck this shit, man. Fuck it all!"[63] Despite widespread evidence of rebellion by residents, the timeless racist myth
of the outside agitator was resurrected once more. "Abolitionists
were the most commonly accused 'conspirators' lurking behind
the Antebellum slave uprisings," tweeted the Midwest People's

History Project. "[B]ecause slave owners couldn't conceive that slaves could organize a rebellion on their own, they assumed that abolitionists must have been pulling all the strings." Early claims of outside agitators in Minneapolis, St. Paul, Sacramento, DC, Houston, and Miami—to name a few—were contradicted by arrest data, which showed the militant street tactics to be largely conducted by locals. Additionally, proponents of the outsider agitator theory have yet to explain how outside agitators can be present in nearly every city simultaneously. Patronizing rumors, first crowdsourced on social media and subsequently adopted by the police, claimed that a single white outside agitator "started the riot" in Minneapolis, as if one person could force thousands to adopt militant tactics when they weren't already good and ready. The parroting of this canard by the Armed Conflict Location & Event Data Project (ACLED) demonstrates the remarkable degree to which even researchers who take great pains to perform objectivity will transparently play stenographers to U.S. police in the interest of erasing the militant tactics adopted on the grassroots level in the early days of the rebellion.[64]

What the label "outside agitator" really means, of course, is anyone who refuses to follow the playbook for "peaceful protest" that limits tactics to a small set of rote rituals that pose no threat to the state. For a time, the George Floyd Rebellion left this pageantry in the dust. "In the over-intellectualized world of the left, where every word is parsed out for meaning and contradiction, what stands out is the clarity of the 3rd Precinct burning," writes Shemon Salam.

> That was the truest event to have occurred on this soil in my lifetime. The people who burned the station down had all kinds of ideas. I do not romanticize them, but I know what their actions mean and say to me. If they had listened to the left, God knows what would have happened, but certainly not the beautiful fires we all watched.[65]

Salam is correct: the same type of professional "peaceful protestor" which would later attempt to lead the George Floyd Rebellion was present on the scene at the 3rd Precinct, trying to stop the militancy that set the whole thing in motion in the first place.[66] And however laughable the outside agitator discourse may have been on its face, over time, and amid heightening states of danger and confusion, it accomplished its dirty work of cultivating mistrust and sidelining militancy.

"The idea that a rupture catalyzed by Black youth could become a vortex for every disaffection," wrote an anonymous contributor to the website It's Going Down, "scandalized the political and professional classes across the country."[67] The We Still Outside Collective pointedly dubbed the idea of coherent "Black leadership" a "white myth." "Isn't it interesting," they write,

> how progressive whites seem to have a direct line of communication with Black leaders . . . ? What's all the more odd is that the voices that they hear from these magical negroes always manage [to] say the same things: "Everyone should peacefully protest on the sidewalk."[68]

Time and again in the u.s., enemies of extra-parliamentary politics positioned themselves as "authentic" representatives of "communities" in order to discredit radicals and convince a decisive number of people, who haven't fallen for this trick before, to get behind the local reformists or else just go home.

In Portland, Mayor Ted Wheeler struggled to repress a locally popular movement, consisting of nightly sieges on the courthouse. As usual, the people taking the most risks to advance the movement were attacked not just by the police but by emissaries of local liberal politics, including those purporting to speak in the name of all Black people. These included local NAACP president Rev. E. D. Mondainé, who, frustrated with his own failure to organize much of anyone to follow him, penned an op-ed in the *Washington Post* capitalizing on the dual nature of the rebellion—both part of the Black Lives Matter movement, and part of a general insurrection against the social order that makes Black lives not matter—to race bait any white people not following his leadership or those of his liberal colleagues advocating piecemeal change through voting.[69]

While Mondainé's intervention was largely a failure on the local level, the problem remains of how people with divergent and often disproportionate experiences of exploitation and oppression—and often different ideas of what radical politics looks like—can struggle together in the real world, without succumbing to the myths that individual people can speak for identity-based categories. This is doubly important in the u.s., where much of society is defined by the enduring stratification along the lines of race. It is undeniable that Black Americans have different experiences informing their politics than non-Black comrades, though even within the former group there exist considerable divergences in experience and political sympathy. In Portland and other hot sites of struggle, these questions were not solved on soap boxes or hubs of online armchair quarterbacking like Twitter, but in practical coordination in the streets, where common risk-taking was the ticket to ride. Militant researchers Shemon Salam and Arturo Castillon place particular emphasis on the participation of "white race traitors" in the rebellion:

> There is nothing more dangerous to the American bourgeoisie than a multi-racial proletarian struggle. And there is nothing more dangerous to the class struggle in the u.s. than the treachery of the white proletariat, which, over the course of its history, has forged an alliance with capital and the state. While the material basis of this alliance is deteriorating, and fissures are emerging, whiteness continues to be the glue that holds bourgeois society together in the u.s.[70]

As these authors argue, while universities and corporations across the u.s. frantically redraft their diversity statements and throw mountains of cash at the antiracism industry, the real fight against racism and white supremacy was in the streets, where people took risks in concert and struggled together to overcome the historical legacy of racism through direct action. As one piece of graffiti on a Philadelphia trash can proclaimed: "To all the white ppl out here with us: you a real nigga!" But this was by no means a unanimous sentiment, as plenty of people stepped up to instruct white people in ornate detail on the proper ways to behave in this moment and thereby preserve their distinct social existence as white. Interestingly, however, while the singling out of white people in u.s. protests is typically done to tamp down militancy, the call "white people to the front" became a means of pushing white participants into more dangerous situations as street conflicts escalated. In the July battle between Chicago Police and front-liners at the Grant Park Columbus statue, "white people to the front" was a call to withstand—and resist—considerable violence at the hands of the cops, as part of an explicitly escalatory action.

Across the country, however, reactionary obsession about authenticity led to tragedy, perhaps most prominently at the Wendy's where Rayshard Brooks was killed. When the restaurant was burned down, self-appointed police informants on social media circulated a video of a white woman purported to be the arsonist, decrying her as an inauthentic participant in the rebellion due to her skin color. By the time she was captured—and it was revealed she was in fact Brooks's girlfriend—nobody could take the video back, and she now faces serious charges. It is unclear if the wannabe cops who circulated her image learned anything. A similar scene unfolded in Chicago, where self-proclaimed anti-cop activists circulated a photograph of a white man dressed as the Joker lighting a police car on fire. Thanks to their efforts, he was arrested and now faces serious charges that will be difficult to beat, proving yet again that not all cops draw paychecks, or even admit to supporting the police.

A similar climate of confusion played out in Louisville, Kentucky, around the killing of Breonna Taylor. Though Taylor's death predated Floyd's, the rebellion lent her case redoubled impetus. In Louisville, an open-air occupation outside the courthouse became the scene of tense armed showdowns with white racists, and a general culture of guns created smaller and more easily foreclosed mobilizations. As argued persuasively in the anonymous report "Breeway or the Freeway: The Rise of America's Frontliners and Why Louisville Didn't Burn," this culminated with a deflated and scattered movement in the face of the city's announcement that virtually no action was being taken to punish Taylor's murders.[71] By the time Kentucky Attorney General David Cameron, a Black Republican, announced the state's unwillingness to prosecute the police who murdered Taylor, reformist liberals had successfully pushed a narrative that the only permissible political issue anyone could talk about or orient their activity toward was the November 3 presidential election.

"If you know anybody in Louisville, KY," tweeted popular liberal pundit Majid M. Padellan on the eve of Cameron's announcement, "PLEASE ask them to stay home tomorrow. If they MUST protest, beg them to please do it peacefully." This message, repeated by many talking heads, seems to have partially worked, in tandem with great state repression, to dampen the response to Cameron's announcement across the country, and most notably in Louisville. Padellan's words were virtually indistinguishable from Cameron's own announcement that, acting "on the side of truth," Kentucky would only press charges against one cop, for a shot he fired into Taylor's neighbor's apartment, and that there was nothing anybody should or could do about it.[72] It was subsequently revealed by grand jurors that Cameron never allowed them to even consider homicide charges against any of the cops who murdered Taylor. Today Padellan seems satisfied that the election of Biden constitutes the movement's victory, although the Justice Department under Barack Obama did not prosecute a single police officer for shooting a civilian in the entirety of that administration.[73]

Those spreading disinformation were aided by a lack of information discipline in activist circles, where outlandish rumors are spread at fever-pitch, often free of factual substantiation, creating needless panic. An effective fabrication pushed by liberal politicians and the mainstream press built on the minimal presence of organized white supremacists on the fringes of these massive street actions to argue that legions of undercover white supremacists were driving all confrontational tactics deployed in the streets. This racist narrative, which denies agency to non-white people and forecloses their ability to take radical action, functions alongside a bevy of misinformation spread by cable talking heads and even supposedly reputable scholars such as University of Chicago historian Kathleen Belew.

Drawing on her expertise on u.s. white nationalism, Belew told NBC Chicago: "When I hear reports of the U-Haul trucks, the [pallets] of bricks left at opportune places, passing out bombs and incendiary devices to people who are already angry during the peaceful protests, those actions across multiple cities indicate some central planning." In one stroke Belew ascribed Black agency to imaginary white actors, while recklessly spreading unsubstantiated—and in the case of bait bricks, debunked—Facebook rumors, which she lent the veneer of her elite institution by calling them "reports." "The evidence for that statement," Belew added to her assertion that white supremacist groups were a major force in the riots, "we have to sort of wait and see."[74] We're still waiting. No matter their sympathies, in spreading such corrosive nonsense with no regard for its consequences, commentators such as Belew made themselves enemies of the rebellion and caused it considerable harm that should not be forgotten. The conservative counterpart to the canards spread by Kathleen Belew and her ilk is the similarly unproven invocation of "Antifa" lurking behind every transgression of respectability and law, echoed by President Trump himself. Even as wildfires plagued much of the West Coast throughout the summer, the product of climate change, conspiracy theories blamed the fires on anti-fascists and warned of their impending attacks on fire-plagued towns. These reports were circulated locally, but emanated from the heights of the federal government, including the Department of Justice and the FBI, resulting in some Oregonians refusing to vacate as fires approached their towns.

Efforts to demobilize from within the movement began almost coextensively with the rebellion itself. Self-styled movement leaders would command raucous crowds, thousands strong, to sit or kneel in the street to listen to meandering monologues, often ordering people to disperse at the end. Kneeling in particular was a bizarre ritual, thoroughly demobilizing (by design or not), and highly inappropriate for the circumstances even in a liberal sense; as participant Tobi Haslett noted: "This gesture echoes Colin Kaepernick, but given the details of Floyd's passing amounts to a pantomime of his murder," with protesters taking the role of Chauvin.[75] For their part, members of the Nuwaubian Nation in Atlanta, confronted with the bizarre phenomenon of self-styled protest leaders commanding the crowd to adopt a vulnerable posture in the midst of an illegal street blockade, shouted for them to get back on their feet, because "kings don't kneel."[76] Rebels in New York City and Portland warned against "swooping," the process by which people with megaphones would emerge amid moments of heightened tactical militancy and de-escalate, seeking to isolate and marginalize the most radical elements of the crowd, which was executed on countless occasions to divert militant crowds into rote activist rituals.

Writing in mid-June for the blog Three Way Fight, Matthew Lyons called to mind lessons from the 1960s and Robert L. Allen's

Black Awakening in Capitalist America: An Analytic History. Drawing from Allen's sketch of how the Ford Foundation intervened in the Black Freedom movement, Lyons offered in bullet-point form a series of forecasts for how co-optation might function in the rebellion.

- They will embrace the language of combating oppression in dramatic-sounding terms.
- They will threaten some (especially local) entrenched white interests and centers of privilege without calling overall systems of power into question.
- They will tend to divide the movement against white supremacy, by promoting or elevating some sections within communities of color, and by exacerbating tensions between radical and system-loyal forces.
- They will be promoted in tandem with political repression, both overt and covert.[77]

As Democratic lawmakers kneeled in kente cloths, journalists scrambled to define the movement as opposed simply to "police brutality" or demanding a more diverse ruling class, and self-identified protest leaders emerged from nowhere to denounce militancy, these predictions were quickly borne out.

For the most part, the organized counter-insurgency strategies we saw deployed were novel only in their scale. In the time since Watts and the birth of Black Power, entire urban political machines have been erected to prevent Black insurrection, with police forces "diversified" and Black and Latinx radicals either bought off, marginalized, incarcerated, or murdered.[78] The post-1968 moment is particularly marked by the growth of the third-party sector or nonprofits as the managers of working-class misery. This was particularly true of the Ford Foundation, which has long sought to fund activists with sufficient left-wing credibility, but who nonetheless pose no serious harm to the balance of class forces. Self-styled BLM leaders, who built a lucrative Black Lives Matter 501(c)3 organization on the backs of rebels risking their lives in the streets in Ferguson and across the U.S., openly pushed to channel movement energy into nonprofit and electoral channels—in other words, the same powers that have failed them up to now. The proximity of these community-based nonprofits to large foundation money and Democratic Party coffers helps them fund programs that offer meager support to working-class people and positions them to broker relationships between working-class residents and employers, landlords, and carceral state officials. Key to this alliance is keeping the peace with the cops, even though this is mostly a one-sided deal.

It is no coincidence, then, that the most confrontational direct action in Minneapolis was taken outside the power of the local politicians, religious leaders, and nonprofits, or that we saw considerably less confrontational direct action where these forces gained control of the movement. In the early days of the rebellion, the task of mediating antagonisms between police and the policed largely proved impossible. Perhaps the only thing many protesters and cops could agree on was that nobody could hold back how they expressed their unbridled hatred for one other. "We're gonna get it on," Muhammad Ali once quipped, "because we don't get along." Not even the most liberal cities were able to control their cops, and all the foundation money thrown at activist circles in the wake of BLM, as a means of purchasing social peace, did not hold back a level of tactical militancy unseen in half a century. For a brief time, the life-or-death conflict at the heart of U.S. society was laid bare. "Action speaks louder than words, bro," a masked Black youth told reporters as they stood outside burning buildings in Minneapolis. "Fuck all that talking."[79]

But it wasn't just the left that could feel the ground moving under its feet. In 1968, Richard Nixon could count on large numbers of white Americans, the "silent majority," to heed his calls for "law and order." Today the geography of recent protests shows many rural, majority-white areas as the scene of spirited and at times confrontational BLM protests. This is significant, since during the past four decades the growth of a massive security and carceral state in tandem with the destruction of the postwar welfare state has relied on the assent of a critical mass of the working- and middle-class white people who form the popular base of the "law-and-order" coalition, a pact with the U.S. ruling class and leading politicians of both parties. The predominant role police play in many domains of social life—education, drug addiction, mental illness, homelessness, sex work, and the list goes on—derives in large part from the success of this coalition, which, alongside the hollowing out of the welfare state, has fueled the rise of what we today call mass incarceration.

Perhaps most importantly, this conjuncture recalls another critical moment of austerity, when the present configuration took shape: the urban crisis of the 1960s and '70s. Just as the rug of postwar prosperity was pulled from beneath the feet of working-class people, a critical mass of white Americans threw in their lot with the forces of police and prisons against the threat of Black and Latinx radicalism. Simultaneously, police and prison guards, as custodians of the law-and-order coalition, were able to secure a comfortable position for themselves in exchange for overseeing the imposition of austerity with brute force. Since then, generations of Americans have seen their pensions privatized and taken away, the public sector being the first on the chopping block of liberal mayors' budgets, community programs offering free services shut down, public housing obliterated in all but a handful of major cities, and homelessness now a widespread feature of working-class life.

Today, even in the most liberal cities, COVID has provided the ruling class with the opportunity to further cut job security, housing, services, and youth programs. Police budgets, on the other hand, are already seeing an increase—no doubt anticipating the fiery potential that a growing immiseration of the working class can translate into. It should hardly surprise us that amid the ravages of COVID, animosity toward the police as the central figure of social reproduction for the American working class, especially its most violent forms, has been on the rise. In New York City, this hostility assumed a catchy slogan.

NYPD Suck My Dick

> Everybody's trying to shame us. The legislators. The press. Everybody's trying to shame us into being embarrassed about our profession. Well, you know what? This [badge] isn't stained by someone in Minneapolis. It's still got a shine on it, and so do theirs, so do theirs. Stop treating us like animals and thugs, and start treating us with some respect! That's what we're here today to say. We've been left out of the conversation. We've been vilified. It's disgusting. It's disgusting.
>
> MIKE O'MEARA, president of the NY State Police Benevolent Association, September 6, 2020[80]

Central to the George Floyd Rebellion was open and bitter hostility toward the police. "Mom, I have to go," a young Minneapolis protester was overheard saying on the phone. "Fuck the police. Mom, OK, fuck the police. I'll call you later. Fuck the police."[81] The classic anti-police slogans "Fuck 12" (numerical slang for police) and "ACAB" (all cops are bastards), derived respectively from hip hop and punk subcultures, have escaped these niche lexicons and become ubiquitous on protest signs, shop windows, city walls, and even cop cars, coast to coast. The most popular chant in New York City—"NYPD suck my dick!"—was driven by Black youth but embraced by all but the most puritanical. "The hundreds of Black proletarian youth and their accomplices who swarmed through lower Manhattan or Midtown each night," writes New York Post-Left, "provided the struggle with its dynamic spark to the soundtrack of Pop Smoke.

They had no interest in formulating demands aside from 'suck my dick.'"[82]

"NYPD suck my dick!" is technically a demand, though the sort that militants don't actually want to be realized. It is a profound statement of the complete absence of common interests between the cops and the people they police. In one swoop it casts aside all the old mindless clichés about community dialogue and all the rest, calling to mind instead the punk band Black Flag's old truism: "They hate us, we hate them," or another anthem from the 1980s that blasted from cars across the U.S. in the summer of 2020: NWA's "Fuck the Police." On Chicago's South Side chant leaders evoke local rapper Vic Mensa's anti-cop anthem "16 Shots" by counting to eleven, at which the crowd rejoins "Fuck 12!" Interviews with Minneapolis protesters in the wake of Floyd's death revealed the growing realization that so-called police reform will not stop police murders, on top of a generalized hatred of the cops.

One young Black protestor in Minneapolis gestured to the fires consuming the Third Precinct as he remarked: "We are living through hundreds of years of discrimination and a bunch of stigma that we face every day. We tried peaceful protesting, we tried every different direction, and this was our last resort."[83] As militant street movements are perennially confronted with the imperative from liberal scolds and other self-described social movement authorities to articulate their content in the shape of demands commensurable with capitalist democracy, we can hardly think of a better response than: NYPD *suck my dick!*

The rebellion's banner victory was the overtaking and destruction of the MPD's Third Precinct. A determined and courageous crowd battled fiercely for hours against considerable police violence, and at last forced the cops to retreat amid a hail of projectiles. According to one poll conducted at the time, more than half the American population believed that the burning of the Third Precinct was justified.[84] This gave the burning of a U.S.

police station a higher approval rating than either of the major presidential candidates. It remains the most significant fact of the entire rebellion that the people of Minneapolis found it suitable to move beyond the usual "nonviolent" political rituals following a police killing and simply destroyed the building where Derek Chauvin suited up the day he killed George Floyd. The Third Precinct was also where Chauvin and his accomplices later filed a falsified story about Floyd perishing of natural causes, which was passed along by their superiors to the press and would likely have passed as truth had the murder not been caught on tape by a courageous Black teenager named Darnella Frasier. One can only guess how many such falsehoods have been cooked up within the precinct walls that the good people of Minneapolis decided were no longer fit to stand. Only the redoubled effort of the Minneapolis Police and National Guard prevented the Fifth Precinct from meeting a similar fate. Tobi Haslett argues, "last year's spate of protests was propelled, made fiercely possible, by massive clashes in the streets—not tainted or delegitimized by them, nor assembled from thin air."[85] And no clash was more significant for launching the rebellion than the siege of the Third Precinct.

Tellingly, the attacks on these precincts contrast profoundly with the events of 2015, when the MPD killing of Jamar Clark spurred a nearly month-long occupation by protestors outside of the Fourth Precinct. The police razed the camp after two weeks, and white vigilantes shot at five protestors gathered there. One vigilante proudly displayed Confederate flags and spewed racist hatred at Black protestors. A year later protestors would take to the streets of St. Paul to protest the killing of Philando Castile. In that year police data showed that, in the area where Castile was stopped while driving, Black residents comprised only 7 percent of the population, but 44 percent of all police traffic stops.[86] After four years of political promises of police reform, the case of George Floyd made it clear that the various reforms touted by local authorities were too little, too late. The resistance engendered by these killings befitted the political moment when they occurred. But we are in a new era. This time around, within three days of George Floyd's murder, the offending precinct was up in smoke. The popular slogan of the Parisian uprising in 2016, *tout le monde déteste la police*—everyone hates the police—far better encapsulates the tenor of the rebellion than clichés about "bad apples," which begs the question of why the good apples don't just blow the whistle or quit.

Above all, the rebellion's anti-police zeitgeist has been aided by the cops themselves. Thanks largely to social media, Americans have seen police use tremendous violence against protesters. Police brutality has also not spared so-called peaceful protestors, even when they are white, nor has meting out brutality been limited to white cops. In the early days of the rebellion the cops' brutal tactics reliably injected fresh impetus to the movement with each new viral video, and the conspicuous solidarity that they show one another as the tide of public opinion turned against them has made the "bad apples" narrative impossible to swallow. For instance, when two Buffalo cops were disciplined for brutalizing 75-year-old Catholic Worker organizer Martin Gugino, the entire riot squad resigned from their voluntary post in protest, making their allegiances clear to all. The histrionics of cops such as O'Meara, quoted in the epigraph above, also revealed the degree to which high wages, enviable benefits, and shameless cop worship across much of American popular culture does not deter the cops from tearfully casting themselves as the *real* victims.

Police unions also fueled the growing polarization by material necessity, since they stand above all else for the freedom of individual cops to wield violence in any way that they see fit, and for the boundless expansion of the police in terms of both their numbers and the scope of their power. By their very nature, cop unions oppose efforts to chasten and downsize police departments, just as they are prone to slander the victims of police violence to help exonerate the killer cops they represent. The head of the Police Officers Federation of Minneapolis predictably dubbed George Floyd a "criminal" and his supporters "terrorists," winning few supporters save for those presently hiding behind badges.[87] Further, as politicians scrambled to pass symbolic concessions to a movement which had them terrified, police and their powerful unions largely proved unwilling if not incapable of budging an inch, besides the occasional "taking a knee" with protesters, sometimes as a prelude to brutalizing them. One of the most prominent features of the post-rebellion discourse has been a far brighter light than usual shone on police unions, and the role they play in perpetuating a violent, white supremacist status quo.

How police unions figured in the election of 2020 is a particularly significant fact, which only added to the redoubled public scrutiny they have received since the Third Precinct burned. By the fall of 2020, an increasingly unhinged and openly racist Trump had branded those within the movement "terrorists," demanded that police "dominate" the movement, and deployed his own de facto militia in defiance of officials in Portland—in between, of course, COVID denialism and an otherwise disastrous handling of the pandemic. As the sinking president was abandoned by much of official society, especially the media companies that had handed him millions of dollars of free airtime in 2016, police unions overwhelmingly endorsed his reelection campaign. This was true even in cities such as New York and Chicago, where the vast majority of those policed were sure to vote against Trump, and likelier than not to be the target of his hateful rhetoric. After Trump's defeat, Police Benevolent Association of the City of New York (NYC PBA) president Patrick Lynch claimed he regretted nothing. For its part, NPR's *All Things Considered* wondered anxiously if this would impact the "legitimacy" of police.[88] We could say that the bigger risk would be the possibility of whatever legitimacy U.S. cops have left surviving its love affair with Donald Trump. But even with Trump out of power, this large and powerful bloc of organized police is a political force that won't be going anywhere any time soon.

In seeking to make sense of the George Floyd Rebellion, it is tempting to imagine the unfolding social crisis as a replay of the 1960s. Thomas Sugrue, whose acclaimed *Origins of the Urban Crisis* explored the complex underpinnings of that era, has cautioned against such facile, if alluring, analysis, and urged instead to look both at the specificities of the present, and its place in a longer historical timeline.[89] We share Sugrue's perspective, and argue that the best way to understand that present in relation to the 1960s is that today we see the unfinished business of that era reemerging not simply as if frozen in time, but altered in profound ways, shaped by the tenuous social order erected to keep the struggle down.

A major transformation since the 1960s has been the rise of the carceral state in tandem with the ascendancy of law-and-order politics as a stopgap response to the crises of that era. This solution has today entered a crisis of its own. Moreover, the rise of a distinct Black leadership class within local governments—"Black faces in high places"—was in its earliest stages at the height of the urban crisis of the 1960s but has since become an *internal* check on political radicalism, far more effective in neutralizing radicalism than external force. Also, the hothouse development of the nonprofit sector—the "nonprofit industrial complex"—as a check on leftism within Black and Latinx social movements has functioned alongside local political machines to keep dissent within business-friendly bounds.

Above all, it is impossible to overstate the social implications of stagnant capitalist growth and the accompanying austerity measures which have played out in the time since the 1960s, grinding ever downward the standard of living for most working Americans, disproportionately so in working-class communities of color. The global crisis of value, through which firms have struggled to find productive outlets for capital, driven to ever more financial speculation in a dangerous quest for returns that manufacture can no longer deliver, has put even the wealthiest countries in the position of struggling to reproduce their workforces, while sewing chaos in the lives of working people all over the world.[90] The accompanying state policies of public-sector disinvestment and increasingly brutal coercion, commonly known as austerity, have passed the lion's share of the crisis on to the people at the bottom of the social division of labor. While austerity has been advanced through the vectors of local political machines and the nonprofit industrial complex, its implementation has rested above all on the weight of the repressive apparatus of the state. The word "austerity," after all, originated as the Greek word *austērós*, meaning harshness, roughness, and an overall mean and nasty modality of life. From Greece to Tunisia, this vision of social life has been contested by popular rebellions. In the u.s. the George Floyd rebellion is the most recent example.

Abolition Takes the Streets

> Abolition requires that we change one thing: everything.
>
> RUTH WILSON GILMORE[91]

We imagine the swirling boardroom conversations and the antiracist training workshops that will unfold over the coming years, even if successful, will only incorporate a small handful of Black Americans into the upper echelons of corporate America and the nonprofit sector. They will also do very little to stem the tide of a growing number of discontented youths who are perpetually deprived of the material comforts afforded to the petite bourgeoisie, and from whom the coming depression will likely strip whatever illusions of social mobility remain possible in the United States. All the while, however, the genie of the George Floyd Rebellion will not be so easily forced back into the bottle.

Today's young people are already the generation most hostile to capitalism and amenable to "socialism." Many found in the streets the means to this end that they failed to win with Bernie's ballot box "revolution." Their political horizon extends far beyond voting or a more diverse 1 percent, but perhaps remains locked in a hazy populist yearning for a better world. An important issue capturing the imagination of these young radicals is the present demand to defund the police.

"A lot of people in the bourgeoisie tell me they don't like Rap Brown when he says, 'I'm gon' burn the country down,'" Stokely Carmichael reflected in 1970, "but every time Rap Brown says, 'I'm gon' burn the country down,' they get a poverty program."[92] The proliferation of police and prisons in the u.s. over the last four decades has been an austerity measure. Despite its widespread popularity, Bernie's plan to reinvigorate the u.s. welfare state through electoral politics ran aground on the shoals of Democratic Party sleaze. Like Stokely Carmichael in the 1960s, many of today's young protestors have learned from the fire of Minneapolis that riots, for better or worse, are often the main pathway to forcing the state to grant real material concessions to working-class people. Before the present George Floyd Rebellion, the last time that New York City was placed under curfew was on the eve of the Harlem Riot of 1935, which forced Mayor La Guardia to consider the city's housing problem and build the Harlem River Houses, a housing project created to accommodate working-class African Americans and Puerto Ricans. Against this historical backdrop, today's protests have moved straight for the jugular of the post-fiscal crisis restructuring: police budgets, which are representative of the hollowed-out welfare state, the material power of police unions, and the base of the law-and-order coalition itself. After surveying a litany of failed liberal policing reforms that do little to reduce police power and growing working-class misery, sociologist Alex Vitale concludes: "The only leverage that remains is to starve the beast."[93]

One of the most significant developments of the rebellion was the overnight embrace by many participants of this previously marginal idea. The defund demand is also an example of how abolitionists within the Black Lives Matter movement have fought since at least 2014 to define the movement not simply as demanding the convictions of killer cops or more civilian oversight of police, but as oriented toward more structural social change, work that prepared the ground for the movement's turn to defunding the police in 2020. After the wave of BLM protests in 2014 dissipated, as some of the activists it made famous segued into the nonprofit sector and Democratic Party, smaller BLM groupings began to direct their energy into local organizing. This coincided with a wave of Democratic Socialists of America (DSA) chapters springing up in major cities, demanding a return to Keynesian economic policy in the U.S. While it is not often acknowledged, the rise of the Bernie Sanders phenomenon, the attendant spike in DSA membership, and the mainstreaming of abolitionism in U.S. left discourse are related phenomena, not so much in terms of one causing the other, but part of the popularity of wealth redistribution as a political goal that has been on the rise since the economic crisis of 2008.

Friends of human emancipation have opposed prisons and called for their abolition for as long as they have existed. While there are prison abolitionists operating around the world, the U.S. tradition draws on this country's particular history of structural racism. The most popular strain of U.S. abolitionism, exemplified by Angela Y. Davis, links the movement against prisons to the anti-slavery abolitionism of the nineteenth century, arguing for the abolition of police and prisons as the unfinished business of the post-Civil War Reconstruction. This wave of abolitionism dates back to the anti-prison activism of the 1960s and '70s, in which Davis took part on both sides of the bars, as the racist cruelty of the U.S. punishment system became a key theme in Black and Brown Power movements, whose members were routinely locked up, and whose ideas found salience with incarcerated people such as George Jackson. As the regime of policing and prisons they opposed deepened and expanded in the 1980s, abolitionists fought prison expansion and police violence at a grassroots level by forming national chapters around the country and working with like-minded coalitions and networks that would become national hubs, such as Critical Resistance. This tradition has spent decades working toward self-clarification, providing an account of what u.s. society is, how it works, and how it can be transformed. It has generated important propaganda, which in today's Internet-driven political culture has become polished and easily circulated using flashy information graphics easily digestible by casual readers.

When an opening presented itself in the summer of 2020, and disaffected people were angry and taking action, abolitionists were well-positioned to provide a sophisticated analysis for what exactly the problems driving rebellion are, and how they can be remedied. This resulted in the victory of Defund campaigns in defining the rebellion, and ensured an attendant emphasis on the political framework of abolitionism. The issue went mainstream enough to become a bugbear of establishment Democrats, who watched in horror as the party's progressive edges committed to defunding their local police and have since blamed the electoral failure of many of the party's moderates on the campaign.

Meanwhile, however, a rebellion that began with laying direct siege to carceral infrastructure became channeled into the halls of power where attempts to downsize police departments now languish and fail. Therefore, while abolitionists were able to provide a powerful political framework for understanding policing as a broader social issue, the remedies that have thus far arisen from the abolitionist toolbox have not only failed, but risk reinscribing the militancy of the rebellion within liberal democratic parliamentarianism, where the rules of the game are fixed against working-class people. We will return to this question in detail in the book's final chapter.

Things Fall Apart

> Last year something massive came hurtling into view and exploded
> against the surface of daily life in the u.s. Many are still struggling
> to grasp what that thing was: its shape and implications, its sudden
> scale and bitter limits.
>
> TOBI HASLETT[94]

After a few months, it was safe to say the George Floyd
Rebellion had run its course. Even by mid-June riots and direct
confrontations with police had largely given way to leftist
rituals: endless marches, kneeling in the street, and seasoned
activists policing militancy to make sure nobody engaged in the
sort of tactics that had catalyzed the rebellion in the first place.
Taken in sum, the rebellion's tactics remained largely street
demonstrations, confrontations, and expropriations. Workers did
not, for instance, take over the capacity to produce and circulate
commodities in places such as factories and Amazon distribution
hubs. Experiments in taking over "autonomous zones" to be
repurposed for non-capitalist uses didn't last very long either;
militant researcher Phil Neel argued that these were a "tactical
regression," harking back to the methods of a previous wave of
struggle, which had been rightly left behind.[95] As the militancy
waned, Democrats rushed to salvage what they could from the
street demonstrations and scrap the rest, while direct attacks
on carceral infrastructure gave way to protracted technocratic
campaigns to downsize their budgets—which largely hastened a
return to the status quo. As early as late June, the rebellion was
already being eulogized.

"The militant phase of the rebellion was from May 26th to
June 1st," wrote Shemon Salam and Arturo Castillon.

> After June 1st the rebellion was not only repressed through
> military force, but politically repressed. Aside from the police,

military, and vigilante crackdown, the uprising was politically
repressed by elements of the left, which reacted to the riots
by blaming them on outside agitators. In some places, "good
protestors" went so far as to detain "bad protesters" and hand
them over to the police.[96]

This provocative prognosis was surely overstated, but it
represented a growing understanding that the militancy of the
early days was not sustaining itself.

There's no doubt the demise of the rebellion was due in part
to the sheer violence that the state deployed to meet protests
large and small across the u.s. But while rebels faced considerable state violence, and its chaotic course surely left many
participants brutalized and burnt out, repression alone does not
explain the limits the rebellion hit. In a society as violent as the
u.s., where brutality can result from simply going to school or
shopping at Walmart, it is hard to believe the cops alone scared
everyone off. On the contrary, it might be tempting to argue that
the demand to defund took the momentum away from the more
insurrectionary side of the movement, thus co-opting it within
the framework of liberal democratic participation. It is indisput-
able that there was considerable counterinsurgency at play in the
rebellion, including that undertaken by nonprofit organizations
speaking the language of abolition, as Salam and Castillon argue.
The question remains, however, whether this was a cause or an
effect: was the militancy of the rebellion captured by left-talking
emissaries of the status quo because the latter are effective, or
because the former was already on the wane? It appears that
voices urging peace, petitions, and poetry were drowned out
as the Third Precinct burned, and only rose to prominence as
the momentum of the original push became fatigued. As rebels
battled cops at the Columbus statue in Chicago, the voice of a
lone street preacher rang out: "This is not the way! This is not
the way!" He was ignored.

The case of Portland, Oregon, in particular casts further doubt on the idea that external factors were to blame for the movement losing steam. There, spectacular nightly clashes raged for months on end, undertaken by a comparatively small, self-selected, and increasingly professionalized set of insurrectionists who engaged in great acts of heroism in combat with local and federal authorities. The impact of state repression there should not be understated, as cops, National Guard, and Trump's federal force meted out great violence for months on end. However, it appears that these provocations were just as likely to energize and swell the ranks of the rebels. For example, the "Wall of Moms" formed by local mothers who put themselves on the line in response to state violence demonstrated the mobilizing effect of police violence. Moreover, the soft side of the counterinsurgency in Portland was by all accounts weak. We have already recounted the failed attempt of Pastor Mondainé to sideline militancy, and it doesn't appear that anyone succeeded where he failed. Nonetheless, the street confrontations in Portland did not add up to a generalized state of social revolution. This indicates that there was a fundamental limit at the core of the rebellion that needs to be considered.

It was both a strength and a weakness of the rebellion that if one were able to pause the action amid scenes of riots and battles with the cops, and interrogate any five random participants, one would likely get six answers for what it all meant. In the hottest conflicts of the rebellion, amid great acts of courage and ingenuity, there was no coherent politics holding all but the smallest pockets of the rebellion's most confrontational tactics together. To celebrate a lack of basic theoretical unity or political organization beneath the daring acts of collective resistance at present is to make a virtue of a necessity, calling to mind Lenin's famous image of "wishing mourners at a funeral many happy returns of that day."[97] While it may feel comforting to blame the demise of the rebellion on the perfidy of traitors and misleaders, the ability of opportunists to get a foothold and derail militant actions, channeling them into the same tired old performances, was not an external phenomenon alone; struggles will always encounter these type of charlatans, and must possess the discipline and internal cohesion to shove them aside.

At a certain point one must pan back from the narrow focus on tactics and think about the politics that will inform these tactics, animate their application, and constitute the social horizon of the struggle in a positive sense—not just the negativity of vanquishing of enemy infrastructure, the imperative to "push the police out, sabotage their bases, sink their battleships."[98] Common struggle on the terrain of street activity produced a dynamism and a shared sense of militant activities, but this is a far cry from imagining the form that a new politics can take when we turn away from what we routinely despise and toward the world we wish to build. By politics, we mean a set of coherent practices guided by a commonly held political vision and an understanding of how actions in the here and now relate to a liberated future. This can be facilitated by traditional political organizations, but need not be, so long as it is accomplished. We don't pretend to be able to solve this problem in writing, but that does not mean it should be abstracted away with the sort of spontaneist smugness that belies impotence in the face of pro-capitalist unions, nonprofits, and political parties inserting themselves into political vacuums and taking over.

Here we have unwittingly steered our course into the harbor of Alain Badiou's philosophy, in particular *The Rebirth of History*. Badiou argues that only a great "Idea capable of challenging the corrupt, lifeless version of 'democracy,' which has become the banner of the legionaries of Capital," can move riots from their immediate context as expressions of belligerence and indignation, toward a positive political conception capable of vanquishing capitalism. Such an idea will not descend wholly from the clouds, however. It must be grounded in an orientation to how people are struggling in the present day, emphasizing the tactics they deploy in their struggles, which constitute the only legitimate starting point for theorizing a revolutionary horizon. Alternatively, to say simply that the negativity of attacking the state will constitute politics, by its very process of unfolding, might solve the question on paper, but the rebellion demonstrated that it is insufficient in practice. The politics that will save the world can only emerge from rigorous theoretical engagement with how people are struggling, capable of theorizing and implementing the bridge from the struggles of today to the post-capitalist society of tomorrow. As Badiou calls for "the rebirth of the Idea," we call for the rebirth of far-sighted praxis.[99]

Ultimately the rebellion was not defeated by external forces alone but succumbed to its own internal limits: a lack of cohesion, self-understanding, and direction. In other words, it was missing its own politics. The u.s. security state is perhaps the most powerful in the world and will not be routed and toppled by disorganized and largely spontaneous actions alone. It is also not inherent that the chaos of rioting and looting, pushed to their limits, will produce a liberatory politics by default, absent of the deliberate cultivation of some communal sense of who "we" are and where we are headed, no matter how broadly defined or deliberately amorphous. Further, the prevalence of reactionary vigilantism, which grew in popularity as the rebellion's power waned, indicated a considerable population of armed Americans who would happily intervene to crush any uprising if sanctioned by the state, as occurred in Kenosha. We find it not exactly lamentable that the rebellion did not quickly evolve into outright armed struggle; this would very likely not have gone well for the forces of human liberation. Instead, the rebellion occasioned the opening of a new moment of u.s. politics, defined by open hostility to the carceral state, rampant illegality, and the recognition that the present state of affairs must not be tinkered with but outright destroyed. Simultaneously, a new generation of militants have flocked to the politics of abolitionism, seeking therein the keys to a post-capitalist future. This is where we now begin.

Despite the radical novelty of much of the rebellion's spectacular scenes, none of this unfolded in a vacuum. To understand its eruption, the forms the struggle took, its targets, and the horizons which it has revealed, revolutionary and recuperative, it is necessary to situate the rebellion in the broader transformation of the carceral state which has taken place in recent decades, even as increasing critical scrutiny has been fixed on "mass incarceration" as a monolithic entity.

"I feel like everything that's happening was supposed to happen," an anonymous rebel remarked, flanked by the flames of a burning building in Minneapolis. "Everything is inevitable."[100]

two

The Carceral State in Context

The George Floyd Rebellion originated as a direct attack on the carceral state: its infrastructure, its equipment, and its personnel. As we have argued, it is a mistake to reduce the rebellion to the issues of police violence, antiracism, convictions for killer cops, or any other of the tropes that reformists deployed to recast the rebellion in liberal-democratic terms. It is significant that while the forces urging a "dialogue" between police and the people they terrorize eventually won out in most places, the rebellion originated with the recognition that nothing more remains to be said between these two hostile parties. Far from procedural reforms or sending a message in the *language of the unheard*, the rebellion was the proactive rejection of an entire way of life defined by the state's reliance on police, courts, and prisons to administer America's racialized capitalist order. The problem is not the administration of police power, or the discretionary power of a few "bad apples." The carceral state, which the cops serve as low-level custodians, is inextricable from the capitalist division of labor and its imperative to treat people as alternatively exploitable or, in the case of working-class Black people such as George Floyd, disposable.

The carceral state is most distinctly identified with the rise of mass incarceration. Sociologist David Garland coined the term "mass incarceration" to call attention to the distinct size,

scope, and racial disparity of incarceration in the United States.[1]
According to the Prison Policy Initiative, a think tank dedicated
to research and advocacy on "overcriminalization," there are
2.3 million people in in 1,833 state prisons, 110 federal prisons,
1,772 juvenile correctional facilities, 3,134 local jails, 218 immigration detention facilities, and 80 Indian Territory jails as well
as in military prisons, civil commitment centers, and state psy-
chiatric hospitals in the u.s.[2] The United States has by far one of
the highest incarceration rates in the world, with an estimated
1 in every 108 American adults incarcerated in jails or prisons.[3]
Profound racial disparities characterize who is incarcerated:
1 in 15 African American men is incarcerated, 1 in 36 Latinx men,
compared to 1 in 106 white men.[4]

As the coronavirus threw into sharp relief the structural
violence and uncertainty that shape the daily lives of 2.3 million
incarcerated people in the u.s., it also underscored the porous
boundaries of the prison wall, through which the entire country
has become an open-air theater of punishment and control.
Michael Tyson's incarceration and death in Rikers Island is
a case in point.

The 53-year-old from the Bronx was arrested in February
2020 on a technical violation: he missed an appointment with
his parole officer. The guards at Rikers flatly refused to take
COVID seriously. "Coronavirus is just a common cold. That's it!" a
deputy warden told a group of prisoners in late March, when they
demanded masks, sanitizer, and cleaning supplies—which they
had to wage a strike action to secure.[5] In early April, Tyson was
among a small number of detainees whom the Legal Aid Society
represented in a lawsuit demanding their release due to their high
risk of mortality from COVID.[6] As he waited for a final decision
on his case, Tyson contracted the virus and died, the first known
COVID casualty in the NYC carceral system. Unfortunately, Tyson is
not remarkable for having contracted COVID in jail. A recent study
argues that over the summer months of 2020, mass incarceration

led to more than half a million additional COVID-19 cases nation-wide, or about one in eight new cases.[7] But how he got to jail is instructive. Tyson's case represents a common feature of the American punishment system, wherein criminal justice agencies such as probation and parole designed as alternatives to incarceration serve as draconian agents of control outside prison walls, and often lead their "clients" right back behind bars. How did this system come to be?

In this chapter, we take a step back to analyze the growth of the carceral state that was the principal target of the George Floyd Rebellion, and which entraps millions of Americans each year in a cycle of stigma, criminalization, and punishment. Criminologists, politicians, and bourgeois media argue that the punishment system is a response to crime. Yet this view obscures the role of state power to achieve a social order amenable to bourgeois sensibilities and interests, and ultimately, to the accumulation of capital. As policing scholar Mark Neocleous reminds us, "the genius of liberalism was to make the police appear as an independent, nonpartisan agency simply embracing the law and protecting all citizens equally from crime."[8] The George Floyd Rebellion briefly shattered the myth that the law is about justice and not about order. Beneath the mythology of policing and prisons lies the reality that these institutions have been used to manage the working class and maintain bourgeois social order since the days of capitalism's infancy. The recent growth of the American carceral state can be located in the particular reconfiguration of political economy and social relations of the late twentieth century: deindustrialization, the growth of what Marx called the surplus populations of unemployed and under-employed workers structured along racial lines, and the state's response to both the crunch of global capitalist crisis and the threat of proletarian revolution which had reared its head in the 1960s. This resulted in an undeniably racialized set of policies that form the basis of the carceral state.

At the time of his death George Floyd was, alongside millions of other Americans, unemployed and looking for work. The COVID recession accelerated deepening inequalities and insecurities that have been unfolding for the past four decades. The financial crisis in 2008 made the stagnant U.S. economy visible, shattering any illusions about its strength. In the immediate aftermath, the unemployment rate in the U.S. climbed to 10 percent, double that of the previous year.[9] Since then, both political parties have made job creation the central plank of their electoral campaigns. Yet the jobs that have since been created are mostly low-wage, part-time work, leading to the phenomenon of what researchers call "jobless recovery."[10] To make sense of why our era is defined by deepening insecurity, many have turned to the idea that automation has rendered many jobs obsolete. However, as Aaron Benanav and Jason Smith argue, simply blaming automation elides deeper and more significant transformations in the global economy: namely the entrenchment of deindustrialization and low labor demand, which has expanded the informal economy and other forms of nonstandard employment worldwide.[11] The result of these transformations over the past four decades has been the growth of a permanent underclass, or relative surplus population, defined by the economy as workers who are not needed with any consistency.

"They have been forced to live there, in all the filth and degradation," writes Chester Himes, describing a Harlem eviction in the 1969 novel *Blind Man with a Pistol*, "until their lives have been warped to fit, and now they were being thrown out. It is enough to make a body riot."[12]

As Himes penned these words, rebellions shook American cities and demonstrated to bourgeois society the political power of this forgotten sector of society. The Kerner Commission, convened to study the phenomenon, characterized the "typical rioter" as someone "usually underemployed or employed in a menial job."[13] The riots were a symptom of the profound economic, political, and social transformations in American capitalism that pushed Black workers outside of the formal labor force and enclosed them into segregated and dilapidated housing and subpar schools. The brutality of daily life in inner-city neighborhoods across America was tightly regulated by the police. The term "underclass" was widely used to make sense of why, for some people, poverty would remain a permanent condition. Liberals cast the underclass as a product of blocked opportunities (like education, housing, and employment), whereas right-wing demagogues like Charles Murray focused on their moral failings and dysfunctions which he claimed were hereditary. On August 29, 1977, the cover of *Time* magazine featured a drawing of a group of Black and Latinx city residents under the heading "minority within a minority" and went on to describe working-class people of color living in America's cities "as more socially alien and more hostile than almost anyone had imagined."[14]

In much of white society, this "underclass" was depicted *as a race apart* from hard-working white Americans. A year after the *Time* story, sociologist William Julius Wilson published *The Declining Significance of Race* to challenge this racist assumption, offering an exhaustive account of how deindustrialization in particular negatively affected inner-city Black communities, sharpening the class differences and trapping a large portion in extreme poverty.[15] Nevertheless, the structural reasons that excluded black workers in particular from the labor market were forfeited for cultural explanations, and by the 1990s the underclass trope became the main way to talk about racialized surplus populations and the new undeserving poor, cast by the media and politicians as those who, unwilling to work, threatened society's moral and economic order. All participants in this often-confused discourse were, however, recognizing the symptom of a deeper structural transformation in the global labor market.

While the term "underclass" is no longer in vogue today, ruling-class fears about the potentially lethal mix of racism and structural unemployment remain. Today, unemployment rates continue to bind Black and Latinx men to the bottom tiers of the workforce. The lowest tiers of the workforce represent the class fraction, or fractions, for whom the carceral state has been deployed, not as a response to crime but to manage daily life, tightly regulating how they are allowed to congregate, support themselves when consigned to informal economies, shop, and even drive their cars. Race, however, is not an explanation for why oppression exists. As historian Barbara Fields argues, in early America, slaves were not oppressed because they had been racialized as Black; they were racialized as Black because they were already oppressed. This does not make the operation of race any less pernicious, but instead invites us to understand race not as a fact of nature, or a prime mover of social life, but instead as the product of economic processes, contingent on both the needs of the ruling class and the resistance—or, in the case of Euro-American workers, the quiescence—elites are met with from below.[16]

Capital Accumulation and Crime

> The law locks up the man or woman
> Who steals the goose from off the common,
> But lets the greater villain loose
> Who steals the common from the goose.[17]

As Peter Linebaugh notes, the anonymous seventeenth-century author who penned this stanza expressed a keen insight into the double system of justice that punished the poor for merely surviving, and looked the other way when the wealthy expropriated, plundered, and privatized land and natural resources belonging to all. During the transition from feudalism to capitalism, the enclosures of the commons for the purposes of increased capital accumulation consolidated the ownership of the lands in the hands of the propertied elite and brutally criminalized displaced people by forcing them to accept the wage labor relation or face starvation. In fact, as Linebaugh emphasizes, it was the state criminalizing the "theft" of wood that was previously free for the taking that pushed Karl Marx to reflect on the dynamics of capitalist social relations and the structural domination of one class by another through the mechanisms of market and state.[18] In his early work as a journalist, Marx argued that the German peasants' willingness to risk arrest to engage in struggles to secure their customary rights to wood amid the privatization of common land, criminalizing their traditional way of life, constituted an important form of class struggle. In the stunning conclusion to the first volume of *Capital*, Marx demonstrates the violent processes that led to the creation of the proletariat—from the expropriation of land and bodies through enclosure and the slave trade, to the foreclosure of traditional means of subsistence by new property laws, the imposition of a mode of production constantly expelling workers into destitution, and, at last, the transformation from large-scale violent coercion to the often-silent compulsion of market dependence, particularly the imposition of the wage labor form, which comes in the liberal trappings of free choice.

"The proletariat created by the breaking up of the bands of feudal retainers and by the forcible expropriation of the people from the soil, this 'free' proletariat could not possibly be absorbed by the nascent manufactures as fast as it was thrown upon the world," writes Marx. "On the other hand, these men, suddenly dragged from their wonted mode of life, could not as suddenly adapt themselves to the discipline of their new condition . . . The fathers of the present working class were chastised for their enforced transformation into vagabonds and paupers."[19] Marx details the genesis of modern property law in a history "written in letters of blood and fire," as the process of so-called primitive accumulation divorced producers from the means of production.

In fifteenth- and sixteenth-century England, legislation beginning under Henry VII classified paupers as "'voluntary' criminals,"
an act punishable by whipping. Seventeen years later, another
law specified that anyone who refused to work could be punished by being turned into a slave for the person that denounced
him as an idler. In England, the bourgeoisie decried pauperism
a "national epidemic," yet neither political party was interested
in ending what had developed into a "highly ramified and extensive administrative system," and sought "instead to discipline
and perpetuate it."[20] According to the bourgeois English parlia-
ment, pauperism "should not be regarded as a misfortune to
be prevented but as a crime to be suppressed and punished."[21]
This history demonstrates how the criminalization of poverty so
prevalent today dates to the genesis of capitalism and colonialism.

The way the state has, in these examples and consistently in
the time since, used the law to criminalize working-class behavior demonstrates that crime is not a natural phenomenon but a
byproduct of society's response to changing social and economic
transformations, including the naturalization of private property
relations as they exist under capitalism. The law is not a neutral
or impartial tool but one that reflects ruling-class interest in
maintaining a social order conducive to accumulation and profit,
thus ensuring the reproduction of the capitalist system as it
ceaselessly—and chaotically—revolutionizes itself. As capitalism
displaced laborers from their ancestral lands, through enclosure
or the slave trade, and revolutionized production and agriculture
to require fewer hands, the punishment system also increasingly
managed growing sectors of the population made redundant. This
is especially the case where workers refused to be passive objects
of history but instead resisted—only to find that the supposedly
impartial laws governing even the most liberal democratic states
can be considerably altered, or ignored altogether, when the
ruling class needs to flex its collective muscle against the people
it exploits. The long history of violent police oppression of labor

organizers, runaway slaves, and other rebels speaks to both the legal and extra-legal applications of state power toward the preservation of class society.

The chaotic reign of capital, sewing pollution, disease, and misery alongside its staggering feats of human ingenuity, creates massive inequality and poverty and encourages and rewards antisocial behavior which the legal system is tasked with moderating. In his 1844 book *The Condition of the Working Class in England*, Friedrich Engels portrayed in visceral terms how capitalism demoralized workers, who were living on the constant brink of starvation and death—a form of "social murder" for which the bourgeoisie is never tried or punished, while proletarians are ruthlessly punished for the antisocial behavior that this condition imposes on them.[22] Early capitalism's assault on the working class was best captured by the evocative prose of writers such as Engels and Charles Dickens, the latter of whom, at the age of twelve, was left to be the primary breadwinner of his family after his father was sent to a debtor's prison. The Dickensian character Ebenezer Scrooge, perhaps the most enduring cultural figure of miserable avarice at the heart of the ruling class, also symbolized the popularity of Malthusian ideas among the British bourgeoisie of his day. "If they would rather die," he says of worker malcontents in *A Christmas Carol*, "they had better do it and decrease the surplus population."[23] Though thoroughly bourgeois in his outlook and rightfully notorious for his disregard of proletarian life, Thomas Malthus understood that capitalism by necessity produced a permanent population of workers for whom there was no use in a labor market. Developing this theory further, Marx noted that capital accumulation produced a population that was superfluous "for its own valorization" and hence a surplus population or reserve army of labor.[24] Marx spends considerable effort in *Capital* outlining the necessity of a growing population of surplus labor, as competition drives capitalism to expel the human element of the labor process—which ultimately creates a falling rate of profit, and cataclysmic economic crises the likes of which states worldwide presently struggle to contain.

By the time the first volume of *Capital* was published in 1867—with its concluding lines depicting the tension between, on the one hand, the expropriated workers hemmed in on all sides by the disciplinary institutions of capitalist society and, on the other, the coming revolt of the working class—Europe and the United States had already erected large-scale institutions to enforce this discipline or else hide away the social problems of widespread poverty and crime wrought by industrialization. In the nineteenth century, laborers thrown out of work and left unemployed or underemployed increasingly found themselves in overcrowded jails and prisons which nonetheless came in humanistic trappings. For example, when Eastern State Penitentiary was built in the outskirts of the city of Philadelphia in the 1820s, it was considered a modern marvel both for its architecture and for the strict discipline of prisoners through "confinement in solitude with labor," purported to inspire penitence, cultivate discipline, and above all, save souls.[25] Marxist scholars Georg Rusche and Otto Kirchheimer, who mapped the disciplinary relationship of prisons to the proletariat in their classic 1939 work *Punishment and Social Structure*, published decades before Foucault's 1975 *Discipline and Punish*, argued that prisons absorb workers in times of low demand for labor, while prison officials ensure that the misery of incarceration is always worse than life outside so as to discipline their captives into accepting the lowliest of free labor vocations upon their release.[26]

Incarceration in early America, of course, only accounted for a small percentage of people held against their will; the system of chattel slavery in the United States had been intrinsic to the nation's politics and culture since the colonial period. It was at last terminated amid a great war, the mass abandonment of plantations by enslaved people which W.E.B. Du Bois dubbed a "general strike," and the considerable Black participation in the

Northern army. Prior to the Civil War it made little sense to incarcerate a slave; corporal punishment maintained discipline without losing precious labor time. Moreover, unlike today's police, the typical slave patrol comprised amateurs deputized by their white skin and agitated by tales of slave revolt sufficient that "the whole white South became an armed camp to keep Negroes in slavery and to kill the Black rebel," as Du Bois puts it.[27]

With the end of slavery, the control of the Black labor force was transferred from the hands of individual planters to the administrative apparatus of the state. In the aftermath of the Civil War, under the control of a plantocracy, the Southern legislatures passed a series of restrictive statutes or Black Codes which limited the freedom of Black people and ensured their availability as a cheap labor force to be exploited for the benefit of the Southern plantation owners. Suddenly, as historian David Oshinsky recounts, Southern newspaper accounts, such as in Mississippi, reported "that 'idle darkies' were clogging the roads, stealing crops and livestock, jostling whites from sidewalks, and fouling the air with 'cigar smoke and profanity.'"[28] As Keeanga-Yamahtta Taylor writes, Black Codes "conflated Blackness with criminality" by punishing unemployment or vagrancy, pressuring freed people to sign exploitative labor contracts, and severely punishing unemployment or any resistance to white employers.[29] For instance, as she notes, the Black Codes passed in St. Landry's Parish in Louisiana stated that Black people could not freely move around the parish without written permission from their employer and faced fines if found in violation.[30]

In the aftermath of the abolition of slavery, freed people once again found themselves on the auction block. Unable to pay the fines and fees associated with the criminal charges of vagrancy, they were hired out to white employers to work off their punishment. While the Black Codes were repealed by 1868, the criminalization of vagrancy continued, and those imprisoned became a source of revenue for Southern states like Tennessee,

Alabama, and Georgia that leased them to railroad and coal mining companies. The onset of Reconstruction brought temporary—and partial—respite from this system of terroristic control. "The slave went free;" writes Du Bois, "stood a brief moment in the sun; then moved back again toward slavery."[31] Reconstruction was ended, as Du Bois argues, by a coalition of Northern and Southern elites, assisted by poor white Southerners convinced that they had more in common with the rich whites who exploited them than they did with Black people who often held the same jobs them. The results of this fateful alliance define u.s. politics to the present day; the immediate aftermath was devastating.

"Once again," writes Michelle Alexander in *The New Jim Crow*, "vagrancy laws and other laws defining activities such as 'mischief' and 'insulting gestures' as crimes were enforced viciously against Blacks."[32] Convict leasing, labor camps, imprisonment for debt, restriction on mobility—all became means by which the formally free Black worker was treated much the same as a slave. In some instances, scholars such as Oshinsky argue, the convict lease system was "worse than slavery" due to higher rates of mortality and the expendability of Black life. However, the mechanism had changed; rather than the private subjugation by the master and a citizenry of amateur slave patrols, the system shifted toward professionalized police and prisons on the European model. While it would take the end of Jim Crow for these professionalized agents of social control to gain primacy over private citizen organizations such as the Klan, which represented the legacy of slave patrols, the abolition of slavery introduced the Black worker as a subject to be disciplined under the banner of "free" labor, not that of the legally rightless chattel slave.

The birth of the u.s. prison at the turn of the nineteenth century was heralded with all the bluster of progressive penology, still seen today, about humane conditions, state-of-the art facilities, and rehabilitation. The hothouse explosion of industry and throngs of European proletarians displaced toward

North America by enclosure and urbanization created a perennial surplus population in need of discipline, particularly of people unaccustomed to the dictates of working for a wage and living in a modern city. By the end of the century this had filled u.s. prisons with proletarians representing a variety of European nations, crammed into squalid and violent conditions devoid of any pretext of social good. From the standpoint of the managerial middle-class that emerged in the final decades of the nineteenth century as part of the professionalization of fields such as medicine, law, urban planning, and public health, this was not only inhumane but an ineffective way to craft a docile and effective working class. This was the primary thrust of the innovations in the punishment system made during the Progressive Era of the early twentieth century, which included the standardization of what we today call alternatives to incarceration.

In the study *Conscience and Convenience*, punishment scholar David J. Rothman describes the genesis of programs such as probation, parole, juvenile justice, and forced incarceration of people with mental illness. "That these measures would expand the power of the state, enlarging the freedom of action of public officials, did not disturb the reformers," Rothman writes. "To the contrary, another distinguishing mark of the Progressive mentality was its willingness to increase the scope of state action and widen its exercise of power."[33] Central to the expansion of these new instruments of the punishment system was the progressive belief in the ability of the human sciences to guide effective management of wayward proletarians toward their integration into the lowest tiers of the workforce. The discernment of the professionally trained expert would oversee the magnanimous application of punishment for the benefit of the individual and society. However, as Rothman illustrates, the lofty designs which undergirded these projects vanished almost immediately, leaving instead a strengthened punishment apparatus that now extended far deeper into the daily lives of the people in its mesh, with every detail of a person's life the subject of punitive oversight, and placed immense power in the hands of figures such as judges and probation officers. Far from benevolent specialists, these tended to be spiteful, small-minded, and severely overworked petty bureaucrats, who could not possibly accomplish the utopian aims of their field, even if they woke up one day and decided to try it.

A similar trajectory was followed by the u.s. police. The modern institution of policing began not as is commonly said in the eighteenth and nineteenth centuries, but much earlier and in tandem with the expropriation of peasant land in Europe and the attendant formation of modern sovereign states. The central figure of police intervention was the laborer freed from the land. "As 'masterless'" people, writes Mark Neocleous, "free from the traditional authority that existed under feudalism, their social, economic, and political condition appeared to undermine social order: as masterless [people] they were considered disorderly. It is in this context that the police project has its roots." The police imperative to regulate "masterless" people, who are formally free and therefore often require compulsion to follow the laws of the market, has undergone considerable mutations over the centuries in tandem with the development of capitalism itself, including the rise of liberalism as hegemonic ideology and the innovation of police practices in colonial occupations. With the emergence of liberal democracies, the rule of law was used to draw a distinction between the acceptable and desirable bourgeois social order "and widespread (lawlessness and disorder) on the other."[34] This has driven the persistent police fantasy that cops and cops alone are "the thin blue line" between order and chaos.[35]

As outlined deftly by Kristian Williams, modern policing in the United States was transformed by three major historical forces: slavery and the informal watch system that developed from slave patrols, the militant workers' revolts of the late nineteenth and early twentieth centuries that saw the creation of a state police force funded by industrial capitalists, and the fears of settler colonialists who sought to protect their interests against Native American and Mexican populations.[36] The Texas Rangers, depicted as heroes in American popular culture, were white vigilantes who aided in the colonial expansion that terrorized Mexican and indigenous people off the land. The irony that the Lone Ranger's sidekick, Tonto, is indigenous is not lost on Native American and Mexican communities, which felt the wrath of white settler colonialism. Nineteenth-century police forces were largely modeled after experiments in colonial rule abroad, whether the Royal Irish Constabulary, which maintained British rule in Ireland, or the Philippine Constabulary, which helped to maintain and legitimize u.s. occupation. The colonial and the domestic contexts of policing converge most pointedly in the policing of indigenous communities, driven off their land by centuries of police actions onto reservations resembling open-air prisons. Indigenous scholar Dian Million charts the historical "double bind" facing indigenous people, "where they are restrained from asserting their own jurisdictions and customs to combat racism, violence, and deteriorating social conditions while the surrounding, non-Indian community is free to criminalize Indians' proactive response."[37]

The racial division of labor in the u.s. upheld by these repressive institutions has developed over time, as have the institutions themselves, most notably with the integration of various ethnic European groups, such as the Irish and Italians, and religious groups, such as Jews, into the pact of whiteness, a cross-class alliance between white workers and their social betters. This historical process has been best described by historian Noel Ignatiev in *How the Irish Became White*, and the work of the journal *Race Traitor*.[38] But for the color line to make sense, it must be defined in relation to what white people are not: namely, Black, Latinx, or indigenous. Simon Balto paints a compelling picture of the racialized history of u.s. policing in *Occupied Territory*. Balto charts the development of the Chicago Police from an institution primarily concerned with policing European immigrants, and combating labor militancy, political radicalism, and public drunkenness, to one almost exclusively focused on regulating the daily lives of Black Chicagoans. This transition took shape as the latter took their place in the bottom tiers of the city's labor force and the former escaped the labor reserve army and ascended the ladder of social mobility through the pact of whiteness, often becoming cops themselves.[39] This is the same social role the cops, courts, and carceral facilities serve today: upholding a racial order that keeps most Black and Latinx people at the bottom, where they make up the lion's share of u.s. surplus populations.

Race, Class, and Punishment

As Balto emphasizes, central to any analysis of the u.s. carceral state is the role played by the color line. While police, courts, and jails were not developed in their European context as explicit technologies of racial domination, they serve as instruments of social control for societies that rely on racial divisions of labor and therefore are especially concerned with regulating the bottom tiers of the social order, which in the u.s. means a racial hierarchy that keeps working-class Black and Latinx people at the bottom. This is a difficult position to parse, especially as an American coming to leftist politics in our moment is often presented with a pitiful crossroads for understanding social phenomena: race or class? In a country that vividly demonstrates in the theater of everyday life Stuart Hall's contention that "race is the modality in which class is lived," this is a false choice.[40] Instead, we must examine the ways race exists as a form of class domination, even if it is not neatly reducible to this relationship.

In the United States and globally, the capitalist division of labor is racialized and gendered. You can learn a lot about a society by looking simply at its division of labor, calling to mind Robert Fitch's famous quip that "vulgar Marxism explains

90 percent of what goes on in the world."[41] A racialized group relegated to the bottom tiers of the labor market is a dream for capitalists seeking highly exploitable labor to use for the worst jobs, and to devalue the labor of the higher tiers. But racism goes beyond labor exploitation. The history of the United States is replete with countless examples of how government-sanctioned policies have facilitated the upward mobility of white Americans and created barriers for Black Americans, and how white people in particular have resisted welfare state policies on the grounds that they would benefit Black people—alongside themselves. Today, popular explanations of mass incarceration in the u.s. center on "racism," and how it continues to be a relevant ordering principle of society despite the end of *de jure* segregation. While such explanations capture the visceral reality of structural racism in the carceral state, they risk simplifying the carceral state to a matter of ideas, rather than seeing it as the result of complex socioeconomic factors characteristic of a global capitalist crisis.

There are not, of course, different races of people. Race is an invented social classification used to stratify people along lines of ethnic, regional, or regionally divergent physical characteristics, on the grounds that these are fixed and immutable differences that divide the human species into distinct subsections. The fact that race is invented does not mean it isn't real; the tragic and brutal consequences of racialization over the past five hundred years, which laid the foundation of today's global racial division of labor, can attest to this. What this does mean is that race alone is not an explanation for anything; as Barbara Fields argues, it is what needs to be explained.[42] Colonialism and slavery did not exist because of race; the merchants and statesmen who benefited from these forms of rapacious exploitation produced racial arguments as a justification for brutal accumulation central to the genesis of capitalism. In the time since, the racial categories produced by this exploitative world order have not stood still, but rather have passed through a variety of religious, scientific, and cultural justifications for the social hierarchies and widespread human disposability intrinsic to capitalism.[43]

A series of long historical developments in the modern world have shaped the meaning of race, have racialized people into categories, and have created a system of advantages and disadvantages based on often ethereal distinctions. The fact remains that, despite transformations such as the end of legal segregation and the rise of a Black political elite in the post-Civil Rights era, white supremacy remains a defining feature of the u.s. capitalist system. Yet, as many ethnicities which were once outside the pact of whiteness today serve as its backbone—the Irish being one such example—we cannot assume the lines of race, or the social significance of racial distinctions, to be fixed.[44] In particular, how the market and the state operate to enforce the racial division of labor, change its contours, and renegotiate its social meaning has changed considerably since the days of slavery. The task that confronts those seeking to make sense of the stark racial disparities of the carceral state is therefore one of following the long historical trajectory of structural racism in the u.s.—from colonial Virginia, through slavery, Reconstruction, Jim Crow, and mass incarceration—without forfeiting deeper explanations for how race is deployed by capitalism differently in distinct historical moments.

A case in point is mass incarceration. Today, many important books and articles have been written examining how race has been inextricably bound up with the punishment system, from the origins of policing to the convict lease system. Nevertheless, despite a racist and brutal punishment system which enforced Jim Crow segregation and upheld the color line across the country, the incarceration rate in the u.s. remained relatively stable between the 1920s and the 1970s. However, by 2010, mass incarceration had reached eight times its historic average of 100 per 100,000 population, further deepening racial divisions in who is incarcerated.[45] So what changed in these decades? The most popular account of the rise of mass incarceration is

Michelle Alexander's *The New Jim Crow*, which has by now been read widely across the country in schools, prisons, and work-places. The book was published in 2010, two years into Barack Obama's first term as president, when much of liberal society was still riding high on the fantasy of a post-racial America. Cutting against this orthodoxy, Alexander argues that u.s. history has been a series of racial institutions—slavery, Jim Crow, and now mass incarceration. In the process, Alexander makes several important arguments.

The first is that mass incarceration is an urgent political problem, the solution of which cannot be delayed or frustrated by piecemeal reforms. The second is that mass incarceration is in fact a system of mass criminalization that targets Black people at a young age, labels them as criminals and felons, and strips them of very basic rights to housing, education, and employ-ment. Third, Alexander incorporated into a study of prisons other areas of the carceral state, including policing, probation, and parole. Fourth, she drew on W.E.B. Du Bois to put a historical lens on the transformations of racial control from slavery to the present moment, showing how the "get tough on crime" era was integral to the overall Southern strategy of appealing to poor and working-class white people, who feared competition over jobs during deindustrialization and grew resentful of the progress of Civil Rights. Finally, Alexander argued that class divisions within the Black community have led to middle- and upper-class Black people ignoring the plight of the millions who languish in prison, focusing instead on civil rights issues closer to their own personal advancement, such as affirmative action.

Michelle Alexander is not alone in drawing analogies between slavery and incarceration. In *Are Prisons Obsolete?*, Angela Davis argues that today's prisons more closely resemble new-age slavery than a modern justice system.[46] Davis uses the analogy between slavery and prisons to argue for prison abolition, which she sees as the continuing work of abolishing slavery. Sociologist Loïc

Wacquant similarly perceives the prison as a "peculiar institution," like slavery, "an appendage to the dark ghetto," which
supplies a steady number of jobless or low-wage unskilled and
uneducated Black workers to rural prisons to be warehoused.[47]
The analogy between slavery and mass incarceration and the idea
of a "New Jim Crow" have resonated with a wide public because
they recognize the enduring forms of racial control to which
Black people are subjected. But, as James Forman Jr. pointed out
when the book first appeared, there are limits to a neat comparison between mass incarceration, slavery, and Jim Crow. Forman
emphasizes in particular the major differences between Jim Crow,
a system that erased class differences among Black people and
treated them equally as inferior to whites, and mass incarceration, a system which criminalizes the most disadvantaged Black
Americans, but allows for a privileged strata of upper-class Black
people who largely escape the meshes of this new system of
control.[48] To make sense of the particularities of mass incarceration, and how it acts upon the racially hierarchized social
division of labor, it is necessary to situate it within the present
regime of state-sponsored capital accumulation, what is most
often called "austerity."

Austerity and the Carceral State

The turn from social spending toward investment in the carceral
state, underway since the mid-1970s was not undertaken in a
political-economic vacuum. The U.S. emerged from the Second
World War as a productive powerhouse untouched by the war's
ravages, and in the driver's seat of global treaties and efforts
to rebuild economies flattened by the war on terms suitable
to U.S. capital. This period saw immense profits, the growth
of the American standard of living, labor militancy among
U.S. manufacturing workers, and expansive social spending,
including the large-scale construction of public housing. While

Lyndon Johnson's Great Society provided extensive funding to the apparatus that would become the carceral state, as Elizabeth Hinton notes in *From the War on Poverty to the War on Crime*, the program nonetheless at least partially represented an earnest attempt to redress structural racism and extend the New Deal to Black America, which had been largely excluded from it under Roosevelt and Truman. But even at the height of Johnson's spending, the conditions of possibility for this arrangement were coming undone.[49] "Until this point," reflects economist Robert Brenner, "the twentieth-century u.s. economy had been remarkably self-enclosed, a reflection of its superior competitiveness . . . But change came suddenly and dramatically in the mid 1960s."[50]

By the Johnson years, the productive boom, and global competitive edge, enjoyed by the United States since the end of the Second World War, was meeting competition from countries that had either built up their capacities from the ashes of war, such as Germany and Japan, or had found new toeholds for aggressive productive output in lower labor costs and weaker environmental restrictions, such as Singapore and Indonesia. Capital, increasingly free of national borders since the end of the war, began its perennial hopscotching of the globe in search of the lowest possible costs of operation, leaving entire u.s. cities that had been built around a single industry, such as Gary, Indiana, in ruins. With highly developed productive forces—or just highly exploited proletarian workforces—churning out cheap commodities the world over, the rate of profit which underlies the u.s. postwar boom, and enabled large-scale social spending, now appears to be an exception that proves the rule of a long historical crisis dating back to the mid-nineteenth century. In fact, as nostalgia for high-waged factory work and "making America great again" continues both on the right and left, it's hard to ignore that more time has gone by since the end of the postwar boom than the boom itself lasted. Nonetheless, the restructuring of state spending undertaken in the u.s. during this time was not preordained by the cold mechanisms of objective economic forces. It played out in the realm of politics.

The postwar period in the u.s., and the world over, was also characterized by heightened struggle from below, led by the anti-colonial revolutions in Africa and the Black Freedom Movement in the u.s., and characterized by intensive street demonstrations, riots, wildcat strikes in factories, and student militancy on and off campus, especially against the Vietnam War. Pushed from below, the u.s. federal government was taking an active role in desegregation and curtailing the most blatant exercises of racism on the local level, especially in the u.s. South. Meanwhile in northern cities, large populations of Black workers who had migrated from the South found themselves relegated by segregation to overcrowded, decrepit, and expensive slums, while the tax base for social spending was eroded by diminishing revenue wrought by capital flight abroad, and the attendant flight of white people to segregated suburbs subsidized by the federal government. Disinvested, overcrowded, violent, and mean, cities became dangerous places characterized by a large spike in interpersonal crime.

By the early 1970s radical critics of punishment sensed that a profound social change was underway and began to explore the relationship between the penal state, economic crisis, and state legitimacy. In the classic text of Marxist cultural studies, *Policing the Crisis: Mugging, the State, and Law and Order*, which he co-authored with four graduate students at the Birmingham Centre for Contemporary Cultural Studies (cccs) in 1978, British Marxist Stuart Hall examined the moral panic over "mugging" that dominated British media in the 1970s to analyze the birth of a new historical conjecture defined by disinvestment in social spending and a "law and order" approach to maintaining social order. Policing the crisis, Hall argued, required clamping down on the "inner city" mugger in a spectacular fashion that reasserted the legitimacy of the state, challenged by its diminishing ability to secure an acceptable standard of living for the majority of its citizens. The popular perception of the rise in crime, he argued, revealed larger public anxieties about immigration, race, and integration. The result was a conservative backlash led by Margaret Thatcher, who promised to put the "Great" back in "Great Britain," just as decades later Trump proclaimed he would "Make America Great Again" by clamping down on immigration.

It is not uncommon in left circles to hear that crime is just a "social construct," and that the data which tell us about the comparative rise and fall of lawbreaking cannot be trusted.[51] This is true in certain instances; for example, it is widely documented that white people consume illicit drugs at about the same rate as Black people, despite the latter being arrested at a higher rate, thus creating crime statistics which suggest that Black people are more likely to use drugs. But in terms of more reliably quantifiable incidents such as murder and auto theft, which are difficult to conceal, the argument that crime is merely a social construct falls apart. Many critics on the left feel that any acknowledgment that widespread criminalized antisocial behavior exists in working-class communities—especially non-white communities—is a concession to "law-and-order" politics or even to overt racism. For instance, both Alexander's *The New Jim Crow* and Hinton's *From the War on Poverty to the War on Crime* emphasize the urban crime wave of the 1960s as a discursive creation of the u.s. right in a way that does not seriously engage with the data or the experiences of working-class people living with victimization. This tendency to erase the visceral reality of antisocial behavior in working-class communities is problematic. It makes leftists unable to have meaningful conversations with people who live this reality, and who are not going to take anyone seriously who tells them that it's all concocted in the imaginations of racist Republicans.[52]

Far from a figment of racist imaginations, by the 1970s, victimization by violent crime was a real fear in many urban

communities across America that were experiencing wholesale
state abandonment. With cut state and city services, underfunded
schools, and deindustrialization that swept away the factory
jobs that once sustained many immigrant and Black communities, young people and so-called unskilled workers were pushed
into informal economies, amid communities that increasingly
struggled to contain interpersonal violence and other antisocial
behavior. When Harlem congressman Charles Rangel transformed
himself into a drug warrior in the 1980s in response to the widespread popularity of crack cocaine and the attendant violence that
accompanied its trade, the rate of crime and concentrated poverty
had intensified in places like Harlem to such a point that many
Black people believed they had no way to keep themselves safe
besides supporting "tough on crime" policies.

Experiencing high rates of victimization, working-class and
poor Black communities appealed to Black leaders to do something about drug sales and addiction. As James Forman Jr. argues
in *Locking Up Our Own*, Black political leaders responded, and
came into power determined to make Black lives matter by ensuring greater police protection from crime as a remedy to racial,
social and economic injustices. While some Black leaders did push
for a more punitive response to crime and interpersonal violence,
others demanded economic aid and rehabilitative measures that
never materialized. The overall response to the violence facing
working-class Black communities was, however, more police.[53]
In a sad irony, while the government has consistently refused to
invest in adequate public health infrastructure for communities
of color, crack addiction became the excuse for massive state
expenditures on police and prisons, rooted in the racialized language of "law and order" and "tough on crime." Behind this was
a new conception of social spending, favoring state actors' decisions to divert state funds away from social spending as industrial
employment declined, and holding the entire combustible compound together with the expansion of police and prisons.

Yet crime is not an objective fact, and crime statistics do not fully capture the punitive response that followed. Starting in the 1970s, a series of punitive policies was passed that shifted away from a rehabilitative ethos that largely kept incarceration rates stable. The increase in sentencing was ratcheted up by the War on Drugs in the 1980s, which led to more incarceration and lengthy prison sentences. For example, Todd Clear notes that in 1972 the median length of stays in prison was fifteen months whereas today it is double that rate.[54] As other criminologists have argued, starting in the 1970s America became more punitive irrespective of whether crime increased or decreased. Commitment to incarceration was a main cause and explanation for prison growth.[55]

It is difficult to draw a direct correlation between crime and incarceration. Instead, it is a complex relationship that criminologists have dedicated their entire careers to explaining. For example, between 1960 and 1972 crime rates doubled before incarceration rates even began to rise.[56] In the 1980s and '90s, "crime rates fell and then rose again . . . while incarceration rates almost tripled."[57] This leads Ruth Wilson Gilmore to argue that the common-sense explanation—"crime went up, we cracked down, crime went down"—is not supported by the data. Instead, she argues, the state should admit that "crime went up; crime came down; we cracked down."[58] By this account, the building up of the carceral state was not a response to crime but rather a calculated retaliation to economic and social crisis, by which the ruling class went on the offensive as it recalibrated the state for a new reality in which fewer workers were needed in the economy. Those hit the hardest would be the Black and Latinx workers at the bottom of the social division of labor.

One thing is certain: mass incarceration was borne out of the politics of economic exclusion and austerity amid a moment of social crisis. A quick glance at increased spending on corrections at a time when spending on other public goods declined confirms the social and political power these institutions amassed in a period of crisis.

As John Clegg and Adanar Usmani correctly argue, policing and prisons manage the working class on the cheap, since the amount of money spent on corrections and policing remains relatively small in comparison to the hypothetical cost of universal health care, universal education, and other investments in the overall social good.[59] They seek to complicate the argument by Alexander and others that mass incarceration can be reduced to a system of race-based social control. Instead they offer a nebulous conception of "economic origins" as somehow distinguishable from the process of racial formation in the United States. The answer they offer as to why the u.s. failed to build a robust welfare state as an alternative to its punishment system relies on the outcome of a "balance of class forces," which the authors argue is distinct from explanations rooted in race. Critics Jack Norton and Davis Stein argue that this abstracts from the racial overdetermination of u.s. politics, imposing a colorblind analysis, and the same old "race or class" binary, under the auspices of Marxism. Norton and Stein name some of those specific *class forces* that did everything possible to squash the welfare rights movement, including the racist Jim Crow Congress, which blocked the expansion of welfare. "Mass incarceration," they argue, "can't be solved by simply bemoaning a lack of social democracy."[60] It is impossible to disaggregate race from class in the United States, as if history is just a math problem with distinct variables. For example, in accounting for the defeat of Reconstruction, which had benefited Southern white people with previously nonexistent amenities like public schools, Du Bois argues that white Southerners were coaxed into siding against the recently freed slaves, to their own detriment, by the white skin solidarity preached by the white elite.[61] This is but one example underscoring how it is impossible to understand the balance of class forces in the United States without treating the color line with grave seriousness.

We must also be careful when speaking of incarceration in purely racial terms. While Clegg and Usmani bend the stick too far, this is the point they are trying to make. While white people are significantly less likely than their Black and Latinx counterparts to be locked up, working-class white people in particular are by no means immune to this behemoth system; white people constitute roughly one-third of the national prison population, and in recent years their incarceration numbers have been steadily increasing.[62] These white people are not, as Michelle Alexander argues, "collateral damage" of a system explicitly designed to oppress Black people.[63] "Many whites—most of them poor and uneducated—are now behind bars," writes James Forman Jr., "One-third of our nation's prisoners are white, and incarceration rates have risen steadily even in states where most inmates are white. That's a lot of 'collateral damage.'"[64] These white people are not the victims of friendly fire; they are living proof of the complex reality of the u.s. punishment system as it functions in disciplining and warehousing the lowest tiers of the workforce amid prolonged economic crisis. The problem is impossible to understand without looking at the role race plays in u.s. society, but is also not reducible to it.

three

The Carceral State Today

I n recent years, reformers have examined the punitive and racist nature of policing and mass incarceration in the United States to make the point that America's punishment regime is exceptional among Western democracies and in the world in general.[1] Befitting America's cultural isolationism, most explanations for the rise of mass incarceration focus solely on America's unique history, in particular its legacy of slavery, and cast the u.s. as unique in its reliance on police, courts, and prisons to manage social problems. Large nonprofit organizations such as the Vera Institute of Justice have relied on this myth of exceptionalism to push for liberal reforms that will bring down incarceration rates in the United States to levels found in Germany and the Netherlands. But outside of a handful of Western European countries, incarceration is increasingly a global phenomenon that shows no sign of slowing down.[2] And so, as the u.s. proved an early testing ground for much of the neoliberal fiscal policy that is now proliferating across the globe, we can observe a similar trend in carceral practices.

The u.s. is, of course, still leading the way. If we were to imagine every state in the u.s. as an independent country, 23 states would have the highest incarceration states in the world, and Minnesota would rank eleventh in the world, just below Brazil.[3] The u.s. incarceration rate (629 per 100,000 residents eighteen years or older) has more in common with the Global South than with Western and Northern Europe. After the U.S., El Salvador (618) comes second in the world for high incarceration rates, followed by Thailand (618), and Turkmenistan (552).[4] But these states are not the outliers; mass incarceration is becoming more the global norm. According to the Institute of Policy Research, since 2000 the world prison population has grown by 24 percent, reaching an estimated 10.4 million people. The total prison population in South America has tripled (175 percent increase) and more than doubled in Southeast Asia (122 percent).[5]

However, U.S. exceptionalism is mostly measured against other Western democracies, namely the UK and the Nordic countries—Denmark, Finland, Norway, and Sweden. While the prison population remains lower in the UK than in the U.S., the numbers have doubled in the past two decades. At 131 per 100,000, the prison rates in the UK and Wales remain much higher than in their European neighbors such as France (119), Italy (91), Germany (70), and Spain (113).[6] Even Nordic countries that have long experienced a form of "penal exceptionalism" have made a punitive turn in recent years, with increases in immigrant detention, policing, and penalization of drug offenses.[7] After the refugee crisis, punitive sentiments in Norway, for instance, have shifted, and "security" has entered public discourse as a central concern. In other European countries, security concerns regarding protests over cuts to social welfare and COVID lockdowns have prompted governments to pass new laws that expand the use of police power in protest situations.[8]

If we look beyond incarceration to examine policing, border control, and other forms of surveillance and punishment, the carceral state again emerges as a global phenomenon. In the United States, the administration of justice is a federal, state, and local affair, with great variation across geographies. Police are the frontline of an expanded carceral net that also includes courts and corrections. According to the latest published statistics by the

Bureau of Justice, law enforcement in the United States is made up of 18,000 federal, state, county, and local agencies with varying legal jurisdiction that can range from a handful of police officers in a department to upward of 30,000 officers. Among states of 250,000 or more people, DC is in first place, with 483 police per 100,000 people, followed by Chicago (483 per 100,000), and in third place New York City (424 per 100,000).[9] However, by comparison with other countries, the size of the U.S. police force as a whole does not particularly stand out. It is comparable to other countries such as Brazil, Turkey, and Nigeria.

Police violence is also a global phenomenon. In the United States, Black people comprise only 14 percent of the population, but 27 percent of those killed by police in 2020.[10] Studies have shown that Black Americans have a one-in-one-thousand chance of being killed by police in their lifetime. But on the global scale, police in the United States are not particularly exceptional in their use of violence, unless one sticks to the view that U.S. society is more "civilized" than so-called second and third world countries. Similar dynamics of race, class, and criminalization are unfolding across the world—in Brazil, Mexico, and other parts of the Global South as well as against refugee, immigrant, and aboriginal populations in Western European countries. For example, in 2019, in Brazil and South Africa police have killed twice as many people as U.S. police. In Turkey, the discourse of the "war on drugs" and the "war on terrorism" has provided legitimacy for an expanding police and security state.[11] In the Philippines, incited by President Rodrigo Duterte's national campaign to eradicate drugs, the police are carrying out extra-judicial killings of unarmed citizens. These police killings worsened during the pandemic, with over 50 percent more people killed between April and July 2020 than in previous months.[12] Globally, police and prisons are increasingly being used to manage deepening insecurity, inequality, and growing immiseration wrought by the disastrous instability of global capital. But as the George Floyd Rebellion demonstrated, in tandem with anti-cop protests around the world, this regime is not going uncontested.

The Carceral State and the Criminalization of Poverty

To make sense of how widely the rebellion resonated, one must understand the presence of the carceral state in the daily lives of millions of people: parolees such as Michael Tyson, probationers such as Rayshard Brooks, and unemployed people such as George Floyd. The vast expansion of the carceral state over the last four decades has also resulted in an exorbitant increase in the number of people with criminal records. A report from January 2018 by Pew Charitable Trusts, a large public-policy nonprofit, revealed that, between 1980 and 2010, the number of Americans with a felony record rose sharply, unevenly distributed by race and geography.[13] Citing a University of Georgia study, the report argues that between these years the number of Black felons increased fivefold, whereas the number increased three-fold for non-Black felons.[14] People with felonies account for 8 percent of all adults in the u.s. and 33 percent of the African American adult male population, nearly double their number in the general population. Some states, including Louisiana, Florida, Indiana, and Texas, have higher numbers of felons than others—more than 10 percent of their adult population.[15]

The control, surveillance, and punishment of the carceral state reaches deep into the most vulnerable sectors of American society: poor, Black, and Latinx communities; the least educated; and the unemployed. Nearly half of all formerly incarcerated Americans hold only a high school diploma or GED and are twice as likely as most Americans to have no high school credentials at all.[16] About 68 percent of all state prisoners do not have a high school diploma, which relegates them to the bottom of the economy. The Brookings Institute has found that only 49 percent of incarcerated men were employed in the three years prior to incarceration, and their median annual earnings were $6,250; just 13 percent earned more than $15,000.[17] But incarceration is only one way this population is harried by the carceral state.

The traffic stop has become the most common interface of Black people with law enforcement, resulting in a cycle of arrest, fines, fees, incarceration, and, in the most egregious instances, death. On April 4, 2015, Walter Scott was fatally shot in North Charleston, South Carolina, by police officer Michael Slager. Scott was pulled over for a broken taillight, and when he walked away, Slager shot him five times in the back. The shocking video footage captured the fears of many Black Americans when stopped by police over something as trifling as a taillight or a de facto traffic offense commonly called DWB: driving while Black. Although many reformers rightfully denounce "militarized police," the daily acts of harassment, disrespect, indignity, and violence perpetrated by cops in the U.S. are overwhelmingly carried out by officers clad in the classic blue uniform, going about the ordinary business of policing.

Not all encounters result in death. A slower, banal violence prevails instead, often taking the form of the protracted extortion of entire Black populations by local police departments, usually in the form of fees and fines. The same year that Walter Scott was killed, a report entitled "The Poor Get Prison: The Alarming Spread of the Criminalization of Poverty" detailed how poor people, especially people of color, face fines, arrest, and even incarceration over minor infractions.[18] It is these more insidious forms of punishment that do not necessarily result in incarceration that lay bare the way in which the carceral state punishes the poor. While mass incarceration has attracted a growing chorus of critical voices, less attention is paid to the daily harassment and extortion of fees, misdemeanor arrests, and probation—all practices that exist in the shadow of the prison.[19]

The Shadow Carceral State

Today, fines and fees are levied against working-class defendants at every turn in the punishment system. While a lot of reformers' attention is focused on monetary bail, and rightly so—bail is one of the main ways in which poor people are taken advantage of daily by the punishment system—the criminalization of poverty is deeply infused into the system at every step, from pre-arrest to post-release. Whereas criminal fines are the standard penalty imposed on defendants after conviction, by contrast fees are automatically imposed and are the price to pay for nearly any interaction with police or courts. Fees are solicited as an alternative to arrest (tickets), during the arrest process (booking and bail bonds), upon conviction (public defender costs, prosecution, crime compensation, DNA evidence), custody (phone calls, room and board, video visits, medical fees, commissary food to supplement the state's meager offerings), and probation (drug testing, anger management, and drug programs). Monetary sanctions such as fines and fees are a burden that falls on poor and disproportionately Black and Latinx communities. They are a prime example of what Katharine Beckett and Naomi Murakawa call the "shadow carceral state," a more insidious form of carceral power that increasingly relies on civil and administrative authority to punish the poor, and in the process generate revenue for cash-strapped cities and localities.[20]

The most common financial sanctions levied by the punishment system are the consequence of low-level street arrests, which are considered misdemeanors in most states. According to former federal public defender and legal scholar Alexandra Natapoff, misdemeanor arrests constitute an estimated 80 percent of state dockets.[21] Every year, criminal courts adjudicate 13 million misdemeanor cases, resulting in significant racial disparities in plea deals. A study of more than 3,000 cases over a seven-year period in Wisconsin, for instance, found that white defendants charged with misdemeanors who had no prior criminal record were 46 percent more likely than similar Black defendants to have all charges dismissed or reduced to no potential incarceration.[22] Misdemeanor arrests can be heard in criminal courts or municipal courts. However, misdemeanor cases like simple assault, trespassing, and shoplifting, along with motor vehicle cases like illegal parking, speeding, and driving while intoxicated are usually heard before judges in municipal court.

Unlike district courts, which also hear misdemeanor and felony cases, municipal courts are more informal and their operations are more opaque to outsiders. There are more than 7,500 similar municipal courts around the country that adjudicate 3.5 million cases each year, which collect over $2 billion.[23] While municipal courts can be traced back to the colonial era, they were institutionalized during the Progressive Era to deal with widening inequalities that were producing vagrancy and as a tool "of strengthening mechanisms of urban control" over working-class people, as Brendan D. Roediger argues.[24] Today municipal courts have become an important source of revenue extraction for cash-strapped cities, as Americans came to find out in the aftermath of the Ferguson police killing of Mike Brown, when politicians and media talking heads tried to make sense of the anger that spilled into the streets and led to looting and burnings of police cars and businesses.

In the wake of the Ferguson rebellion, the Department of Justice carried out a scathing investigation into the Ferguson police department, which confirmed what its Black residents and many around the country already knew about the extent of racist police power. The report found that, despite being only 65 percent of Ferguson's population, Black people made up 95 percent of people detained at the city jail for more than two days, 85 percent of drivers stopped by the police, 95 percent of people charged with petty crimes relating to walking on roads, 94 percent of "failure to comply charges," and 92 percent of disturbing the peace charges.[25] However, another interrelated trend emerged: the Department found that aggressive policing tactics were linked to the city's emphasis on revenue generation—a message that "is stressed heavily within the police department" and which comes from the upper echelons of city leadership. Black people swept up in these aggressive policing schemes are then cycled through the local municipal court, or what Alexandra Natapoff calls "the bottom of the penal pyramid."[26] Municipal courts like the one in Ferguson ultimately expand police power and legitimize aggressive policing practices; they are in fact a stakeholder in the daily extortion of the citizenry. In 2013, the Ferguson Municipal Court issued an average of three warrants per household, and in the same year court fees alone accounted for 20 percent of the city's overall operating budget.[27] This trend points to a strong symbiosis between aggressive cops, who target Black and Latinx communities, and the local governments who rely on this harassment to generate revenue.

The rise of criminal justice fees and fines as an important aspect of the punishment system in places like Ferguson speaks to a larger reconfiguration of public finance as a local response to a deeper-seated fiscal crisis. In the 1970s, central cities like St. Louis experienced an economic shortfall, as middle-class taxpayers fled to the suburbs at the exact time that federal dollars supporting welfare state expenditures were running dry, and the disastrous effects of deindustrialization and capital flight were beginning to be felt by municipalities and individual working-class people alike. The city's neglect and subsequent destruction of the massive Pruitt Igoe housing complex, once dubbed "Manhattan on the Mississippi," came to symbolize its commitment to cutting with the grain of austerity policies. As Colin Gordon and Clarissa Rile Hayward argue in their study of Ferguson, local elites there similarly struggled to raise revenues to pay for infrastructure and services.[28] Property values continued to plummet and local officials failed to attract retail investors. By 2011, fines and fees outpaced property taxes as a source of revenue for the municipality; the entire government of Ferguson was effectively a parasite on its poorest citizens.

Similar trends can be noted throughout the country. A study conducted by the Fines and Fees Justice Center, a nonprofit national advocacy organization, found that while the extent of the nation's court debt is unknown due to a lack of reported data, an examination of fourteen states uncovered an estimated personal debt, emanating from the punishment system, totalling $27.6 billion.[29] In another study, researchers at the Brennan Center of Justice found that between 2012 and 2017, ten counties in the states of Florida, New Mexico, and Texas amassed more than $1.8 billion in uncollected debt from fines and fees.[30] These revenues are often dumped into running courts and jails. For example, in Texas and New Mexico, counties spend an estimated 41 percent of all revenue on court hearings and jail costs.[31] While historically states and localities have relied on fines and fees to fund the everyday activities of courts and jails, the recent spike can be attributed to rising costs associated with mass incarceration as well as the overall devolution of the punishment system, as states pass the costs along down the ladder, until they fall on the individual defendant.

In 2019, Jamie Tillman, a white woman originally from Nashville, Tennessee, walked to the public library in Corinth, Mississippi, to check on her employment applications. She had recently moved to Mississippi to be closer to her son and to find work. She was approached by police officers who accused her of public intoxication and arrested her. Like many Americans she pleaded guilty, believing that the judge would not take her word over that of police officers. The judge demanded she pay a $100 fine or face up to thirty days in jail. She was unable to pay the fine and was sent to the local jail, where her incarceration went towards paying her fees, at a rate of $25 per day. However, she soon found out that a court processing fee was added to her bill, increasing her payment to $255. While incarcerated in the county jail, she met countless other women who were in a similar predicament.[32] Courts like the one in Corinth exist all over America, especially in municipalities and counties that are cash-strapped and looking for creative ways to increase their revenues and increasingly shifting the financial burden onto defendants. For those like Tillman who cannot pay, the result is putative incarceration that can only be likened to that of a debtors' prison.

In many cities and states, fines and fees resulting from a simple misdemeanor arrest can be a significant burden on someone surviving on a minimum wage job. New York is a prime example. According to Vera Institute of Justice, New York state and local governments collected an estimated $1.21 billion in fines and fees in 2018.[33] A simple arrest in New York City can easily rack up exorbitant fines and fees. A 2017 study of 37 residents in New York State found that 40 percent owed more than $1,000 in court fees, or about half of the monthly salary of a minimum-wage worker.[34] Arrest charges add up; the cost of municipal violations is $95, $175 for a misdemeanor, and $300 for a felony, and another $75 tacked on for crime victims assistance and DNA database fees.[35] After thirty days of nonpayment, a driver's license can be suspended, and if someone is caught driving with a suspended license, there is a fee of $633, amounting to 31 percent of a minimum-wage worker's monthly salary, on top of the possibility of a disruptive arrest. According to data collected by the National Criminal Justice Debt Initiative, defendants who are unable to pay fees associated with their offenses can have their wages garnished, driver's license suspended, and, if they default in states such as Pennsylvania, Louisiana, and Virginia, they can even be incarcerated.[36] In September 2014, the American Civil Liberties Union (ACLU) brought a suit against a Michigan court for imprisoning a woman who had fled a boyfriend threatening her with a gun, only to be arrested and sentenced to six months in prison because she was cited for driving without a license and had outstanding fines.[37]

For the people at the bottom of America's racialized division of labor, every interaction with the punishment system, including as the victim of crime, can lead to fines, fees, and incarceration.

America on Probation

"I just feel like some of the system could look at us like individuals," Rayshard Brooks remarked, of his time on probation. "We do have lives. It's just a mistake that we made, and not just do us as if we are animals."[38] Brooks had been sentenced to one year in prison and six months' probation. He was trying to navigate limited options for employment and housing with a criminal record—an experience that one in every three Black men in America shares. Brooks's desperation to make ends meet pushed him to answer a Craigslist ad put out by the nonprofit Reconnect, which sought to interview people about their experiences on probation and parole. "That's a hard feeling to stomach, you know, with you going out and you're trying and by you having this so-called record . . . it's hindering us from going out in public to try and provide for ourselves . . . and getting ourselves back on track," continued a frustrated Brooks. Just months later, on the night of June 12, 2020, the 27-year-old father of four fell asleep in the drive-through lane at a Wendy's on Atlanta's Southside, where he was approached by two white police officers. The police later stated that upon failing a sobriety test, he attempted to flee.

While we do not know why Brooks ran from the cops, it is difficult not to assume that it had to do with the fear that a DUI (driving under the influence) arrest would be a violation of his probation and would send him back to prison. One of the cops shot the fleeing Brooks three times and killed him. Brooks's murder came on the heels of the George Floyd Rebellion and after two Atlanta police officers were charged with the forceful arrest of two college students sitting in their car during a nearby Black Lives Matter protest. Less than 24 hours later, Atlanta police chief

Erika Shields resigned. Amid Mayor Bottom's speech accepting Shields's resignation and calls to terminate officer Rolfe, a crowd of 1,000 protestors gathered at the Wendy's, and it was set afire. Brooks's senseless death illustrates the relationship between policing, probation, parole, and mass incarceration. Ironically, we know his thoughts on the system, thanks to Reconnect, which provides technology to probation and parole officers to monitor their "clients" on the cheap.

According to data gathered by the Robina Institute, the probation supervision rate in all fifty states in the United States is more than five times the average of all European countries. Between 1980 and 2010 alone, the rates of people on probation and parole in the United States increased fourfold in tandem with growing incarceration rates. Today, a greater share of the American population is under probation and parole than incarcerated: 1 in every 55 Americans.[39]

"[Probation] took all my money, kept me incarcerated for simple little mistakes. It's really been a lot of pain," one probationer in Georgia told researchers from Human Rights Watch and the ACLU.[40] He pleaded guilty to probation in the hope of avoiding prison, but once he failed to pay some fines, relapsed, and started using drugs, he found himself back in prison. His experiences reveal a growing and disturbing trend in probation today: the advent of "offender-funded probation," which refers to states and localities that charge defendant fees and fines to help finance the cost of running supervision. According to the report, despite a Supreme Court ruling (*Bearden vs Georgia*) in 1983, the State of Georgia and a handful of other states in the country are putting people on probation to make them pay court fines and fees. The transformation of probation into a debt collection tool is referred to as "pay only" probation, which targets the poorest and most vulnerable Americans, because the poorer you are, the greater the struggle to pay fees and fines, the longer the probation sentence, and the greater the threat of incarceration.

This report also found that many people locked up for supervision violations were not convicted of committing a new offense but were instead punished for breaking the rules of their supervision. Something as simple as not reporting an address change to a probation officer often led to reincarceration. The conditions of probation are wide ranging and can include the following: obey all state and local laws, report regularly (often weekly) to the probation officer, report any changes of employment or address, follow court-mandated mental-health or drug-treatment programs, find and maintain regular employment, abstain from the use of alcohol or drugs and submit to regular testing of controlled substances, do not possess firearms or other dangerous weapons, conform to electronic monitoring or special curfews, refrain from travel outside the jurisdiction without prior permission of the probation officer, pay court-ordered and supervision fees, and avoid certain people (especially those with criminal records) and places. While local jurisdictions have their own standard conditions that apply to all probationers and parolees, courts can also add "discretionary" conditions that they deem appropriate, constituting complex and highly subjective punishment system interventions into a person's life, for behaviors and habits that are not against any law. If a probationer is in violation of any of the conditions, which are quite difficult and for some people impossible to observe, their probation can be revoked, and they can end up in jail. The threat of incarceration looms large for those on probation and parole, especially given the length of probation sentences. For example, in Wisconsin, Pennsylvania, and Georgia probation terms can exceed ten years, reaching twenty, and even life.

Probation supervision, like mass incarceration, tends to be concentrated among the most economically disadvantaged and racialized populations. Prison Policy has found that an estimated two thirds of those on probation make less than $20,000 a year. While African Americans comprise 13 percent of the u.s. population, they are 30 percent of those under community supervision.[41]

Using household surveys for the years 2010, 2011, 2012, and 2014, Michelle Phelps found that, similar to the prison population, "the probation population is significantly skewed towards young men of color with low levels of formal education."[42] One in six Black men without a high-school diploma reported being on probation during the years studied. The lack of education and poverty exacerbates the added financial burden probation imposes on poor defendants.

One of the standard conditions of probation and parole is that people are required to pay court fees, criminal fines, one-time fees, monthly supervision fees, electronic monitoring costs, or some combination of any of these, and/or restitution to alleged victims. In many states, probationers and parolees also have to pay for their rehabilitation. In New Mexico, monthly supervision fees can range anywhere from $25 to $150, which are unaffordable for 83 percent of probationers, who make less than $20,000 a year.[43] In Alameda County, California, supervision fees for the average adult on probation are more than $6,000. In 2009, on the heels of the recession, the Alameda County Board of Supervisors increased fees for probation supervision from $30 to $90 per month and imposed additional new fees, demonstrating yet again how cash-strapped localities pass the costs of administering the punishment system onto individuals and their families.[44] In 1990, only 26 states charged offenders for probation and parole supervision. By 2014, this had increased to 44 states.[45]

In 2017, the ACLU filed a federal lawsuit challenging the illegal arrest and incarceration of poor people in Lexington, South Carolina. Impoverished residents, disproportionately Black and Latinx, who cannot pay traffic fines and misdemeanor fees, are locked up in Lexington County Detention Center. One of the plaintiffs, Twanda Marshinda Brown, was incarcerated for 57 days because she could not afford to pay the entire $1,907.63 that she owed.[46] The Vera Institute of Justice calls fines and fees an "intermediate sanction"[47]—an example of a noncriminal penalty that does not result in jail time or probation. Yet its own data shows otherwise. Oftentimes nonpayment of such noncriminal fines and fees results in incarceration. For example, Vera researchers found that in 2017 New York City officials issued 11,000 warrants for nonpayment of fees and 161 people spent time in jail.[48] Prison Policy estimates that 10.6 million people cycle through local jails in the United States each year, no doubt due to inability to pay bail, fees, and fines.[49]

The extortion of low-income defendants is popularized by such shows as *Dog the Bounty Hunter*, which glorifies the bail bond industry by depicting the show's hero chasing down people who had violated their bail in a manner reminiscent of the pro-police exploitation show *Cops*. The bail industry is an important player in the resistance to reform the cash-bail system, but focusing on this racket alone leaves untouched the ways in which municipal courts also take advantage of the poor. The reality is that, despite the ways in which fines, fees, and bail have made police, probation, courts, and bail bondsman into hunters, many counties and municipalities often lack the capacity to collect the debt, so they let it accrue and continue to pile on late fees instead of using swift punishment for nonpayment. In 2017, for instance, New York City courts collected nearly half of the surcharges imposed on defendants, an estimated $6.5 million of the $18 million owed.[50] This has more egregious consequences, since it keeps poor Americans in a never-ending cycle of poverty and incarceration.

The rise of fines and fees, privatized probation practices, and new technologies of surveillance and social control such as electronic monitoring and so-called risk assessment reveal not only the carceral state's attempt to control and repress surplus populations, but how the punishment system is increasingly being privatized. This commodification has been aided by processes of carceral devolution, which offloads the power to punish and "rehabilitate" onto third-party organizations.[51] As Maya Schenwar

due to criminal history. As a result, in many locations studied, Black probationers were revoked at higher rates than their white counterparts. These findings support the findings of other researchers on racial disparities in mass supervision which has found that Black defendants are revoked at higher rates.[63]

The vast system of probation and community supervision demonstrates that the carceral state is not reducible to the prison. Large swaths of the u.s. social terrain are being repurposed to manage the social effects of capitalist crisis, by offsetting the worst of the crisis onto our society's most powerless people, using an ever-widening nexus of punishment and control. While these measures have succeeded to some degree in mitigating social crisis and foreclosing large-scale rebellion since the early 1970s, they are ultimately stopgap measures which do not solve the contradictions, intrinsic to capitalism itself, to which they respond. Therefore, their demise is only a matter of time. In recent years we have seen cracks appearing in the foundation of the carceral state, namely through a deepening crisis of legitimacy surrounding not only its brutal role in maintaining the u.s. social order, but the sheer cost of it all, which gives new meaning to the old bugbear of "big government." The space opened up by this crisis of legitimacy has been inhabited by both radicals and reformers. We will turn to the solutions offered by radicals in the final chapter. First, it is necessary to look at the work of reformers: those who want to rescue the capitalist social order from the crisis of the carceral state.

four

The Limits of Reform in the Era of Austerity

Do I look like a radical socialist with a soft spot for rioters? Really?

JOE BIDEN, on the campaign trail in Pittsburgh[1]

The George Floyd Rebellion was the latest in a global avalanche of anti-police, anti-government, and anti-austerity protests that led Endnotes to claim with some certainty: "The insurrection is not coming, it has already arrived, unfolding on a planetary level with greater and greater intensity every year."[2] The legitimacy and hegemony crises facing global capitalism have been an important subject for leftists and radicals who imagine a universalist drive of global capitalism toward authoritarianism as the main ruling-class response to the structural conditions of global capitalism. For instance, William Robinson's new book, *The Global Police State*, makes a compelling argument about how the deepening capitalist crisis and growing surplus populations are leading the transnational ruling class to embrace greater repression via policing, mass incarceration, border control, and warfare.[3]

Certainly, global developments such as the draconian response to the flood of refugees and the rise of right-wing ethnonationalism seem to substantiate his argument. However, as Robinson also recognizes, while some parts of the transnational capitalist ruling class would like nothing more than to expand policing and repression, reformist tendencies within the same class are quite vocal about their support of global Keynesianism as a solution to the persistent levels of social unrest and growing inequality. This period of unstable and crisis-driven capital accumulation has been described by Dave Ranney as "churning and flailing," as the ruling class attempts to reorganize capitalism to restore profits, largely relying on financialization and austerity, but is increasingly met with resistance from below.[4] The rise of a massive punishment system has been central to the imposition of austerity in the United States. It is therefore important to pay attention to the crisis of legitimacy engulfing this system, as seen in local rebellions and movements like Black Lives Matter but also within the ruling class itself, which is breaking ranks on the question in surprising ways.

In this chapter, we focus on how the bipartisan consensus to reform the carceral state has muddled the terrain of anti-carceral struggle by adopting radical concepts and rhetoric to push for building a more efficient punishment, which nonetheless upholds the same brutal social order that has for decades been propped up by mass incarceration. We call particular attention to the way that the desperate imperative to relieve the misery caused by the punishment system can be weaponized by the ruling-class to provide a necessary corrective to a system in crisis, thereby protecting capitalism in the long term, under the auspices of "social justice."

The Politics of Punishment

The George Floyd Rebellion made evident the growing chasm between a critical mass of Americans who demonstrated their rejection of the status quo by attacking carceral infrastructure or staging illegal protests against the police on the one hand, and on the other hand, a well-funded and entrenched bipartisan consensus bent on managing the crisis and recuperating the moment towards a healthier punishment system in the long term. Even as Democrats and Republicans alike decried the most courageous participants in the George Floyd Rebellion as violent rioters intent on ripping apart the very fabric of American democracy, they couldn't balk on the issue of so-called criminal justice reform. Due in no small part to the threat of more rebellions, beginning in 2016 opposition to the 1994 Crime Bill became an important litmus test for the Democratic Party's ability to do well by its Black and Latinx constituents. This demonstrates how much the political terrain has changed in just the last two decades, driven by revolt from below.

The significance of this policy reversal cannot be overstated. The 1994 Violent Crime Control and Law Enforcement Act, commonly called the Crime Bill, is widely cited by anti-prison activists as one of the main causes of the rise of mass incarceration. It provided more than $30 billion in federal spending over a span of six years for state and local law enforcement, crime prevention programs, and the construction of new state prisons. It also increased federal penalties for many crimes, authorized the death penalty for existing and new federal crimes, and instituted federal "three-strikes-you're-out" laws. The bill affirmed the Democratic Party's support for the idea of being "tough on crime," an issue they sought to wrest away from the Republicans. In the 1990s the bill was without serious challenges on either side of the political aisle. But by 2020, it had few defenders, with both major presidential candidates disavowing it and citing its impact on Black America in particular.

This was the denouement of a long historical arc. In the 1980s and '90s, Republican presidential success relied on scaremongering about crime and disorder. Richard Nixon sponsored ads of cities burning, Reagan launched the "War on Drugs," and in 1988 George Bush Sr. ran the infamous Willie Horton ad to attack his opponent Michael Dukakis as being "soft on crime." In a hyper-punitive national climate, Dukakis's public opposition to the death penalty ruined any chances he had to win against Bush. In 1994, conservative Republicans sought to further unify their party around the "Contract with America" advocated by Minority Whip and Georgia Representative Newt Gingrich, which stipulated more funding for prison construction, tougher "truth-in-sentencing" laws, and more police officers in the streets and public schools. In the run-up to the election in 1992, Democratic Party candidate Bill Clinton decided he could not afford to be seen as "soft on crime." While governor of Arkansas, Clinton had undergone a profound conversion, from a staunch opponent to a supporter of the death penalty. The cause was no moral revelation, however, but his electoral loss to a Republican candidate. Hell-bent on winning the election in 1992, Clinton left the campaign trail to return to Arkansas to oversee the high-profile execution of Ricky Ray Rector, a mentally ill Black man. During his campaign, Clinton continued to brag about his support for the death penalty and restrictions on welfare recipients. The Democrats' embrace of "tough on crime" signaled the party's shift to the right. By the end of Clinton's second term, law and order was a bipartisan consensus.

Today, this political terrain has shifted considerably. After decades of bipartisan support for "tough on crime" policies that encouraged mass incarceration and expanded police power, both parties have incorporated so-called criminal justice reforms into their platforms. Even Republicans have weakened their tough-ness on crime, as mass incarceration has become too costly. A few months before the police killings of Philando Castile and Alton Sterling, in April 2016 the Republican National Committee passed a resolution calling for the overhaul of the country's pun-ishment system, beginning with reducing the size of its prisons.[5] Even as they revised the resolution in the wake of police deaths in Dallas and Baton Rouge, to express strong support for law enforcement, the platform remained committed to reforms such as increased use of alternatives to incarceration and modifications to mandatory minimum sentencing. The Democratic Party platform was far more radical in its rhetoric, calling for the "end of mass incarceration" and the death penalty, reform of mandatory minimum sentencing, and the cessation of the school-to-prison pipeline. Four years later, in the run-up to the presidential election, Joe Biden, once the architect of the 1994 Crime Bill, pledged to voters in South Carolina that if elected he would cut incarceration by half, which had long been a goal of liberal reform organizations such as the American Civil Liberties Union (ACLU).

The past decade has also seen significant criminal justice reforms, including decriminalization of marijuana possession in 27 states and the District of Columbia; decreases in state prison populations in a handful of states including Alabama, California, Connecticut, New Jersey, New York, Rhode Island, and Vermont; the election of progressive prosecutors in San Francisco, Philadelphia, Detroit, Chicago, and a handful of other states across the country; the overhaul of California's cash bail system and its demise in Illinois (the first in the nation); and the restoration of voting rights to people with felonies in eighteen states. Are we witnessing *the end of mass incarceration*?

Unfortunately, these bipartisan legislative efforts are doing very little to chip away at the carceral state. They are driven largely by austerity, and amount to nothing more than a political shell game where the state's reliance on policing, jails, and prisons is not reduced as much as displaced elsewhere. However, they pose a significant challenge to abolitionist organizing because they are adopting the rhetoric of decarceration—a "strategic launchpad for the politics of abolition," as abolitionist Dan Berger puts it, and a term often synonymous with prison abolition—in order to expand carceral power, not reduce it.[6]

A notable example of the challenges that unfold when ruling elites embrace decarceration is California's realignment experiment. As Ruth Wilson Gilmore argues in *Golden Gulag*, beginning in the 1980s, California embarked on the largest prison building project in America's history, the consequence of right-wing politicians and voters confronting the crisis of widespread unemployment attendant to deindustrialization with a punitive solution. In response to the growth of this prison system, activist groups and organizations ranging from abolitionists to more established nonprofit organizations mobilized for the cessation of prison construction, the closure of prisons, and the diversion of resources thereby saved into communities most impacted by mass incarceration. The state widely resisted decarceration efforts until it was forced to do so by the Supreme Court ruling *Brown vs Plata* in 2011, which required California to reduce the prison population, and release at least 30,000 prisoners in the next two years. Suddenly state politicians embraced decarceration as a necessary evil. But this did not simply mean freeing people from the meshes of the carceral net.

Some reformers were optimistic that state officials had been moved to reduce prison populations by humanitarian concern about horrific prison conditions, including overcrowding and a lack of mental health and physical care. After all, it was a prisoner-led class action lawsuit in 2007 that called mainstream attention to the problem of overcrowding inside California's prisons and proved that California DOC's renaming to Department of Corrections and Rehabilitation two years prior was a farce. Over the course of four years, the lawsuit made its way to the Supreme Court, which decided that prison overcrowding was the "primary" reason for lack of medical care, a violation of the Eighth Amendment, prohibiting the use of cruel and unusual punishment.[7] By that time, California prisons were operating at 200 percent overcapacity; conditions were dismal and prison officials could not even meet the most minimum of health standards. To comply with court-ordered decarceration, Governor Jerry Brown signed Assembly Bill 109, called the Public Safety Realignment Initiative, commonly referred to as "realignment." Suddenly, all eyes were on California's realignment experiment, which was heralded as a stepping stone towards decarceration and, most significantly from the state's perspective, saving $2 billion annually. Three years later in 2014, the bill Proposition 47, a ballot initiative cast by more than 60 percent of Californians, was passed, which reduced many felony nonserious and nonviolent property crimes into misdemeanors.

At last, there seemed to be political willpower and popular support for decarceration. However, instead of closing down prisons and releasing incarcerated people, this new set of policies simply shifted the responsibility for monitoring, supervising, and punishing low-level offenders from state prisons to county custody. California's realignment "follows to the letter devolution's underlying principles," by offloading the responsibility to manage and punish working-class people to local county agencies.[8] As a result, incarceration was reshuffled from the state to local county jails and expanded the use of alternatives to incarceration programs, including probation, house arrest, and so-called flash incarceration. California's decarceration efforts reveal a set of political decisions motivated not by humanitarian efforts to improve prison conditions but an effort to reduce prison costs. It offers a clear example of what activist scholars Kay Whitlock and Nancy A. Heitzeg term the "carceral con," to describe how contemporary bipartisan criminal justice reforms are actually expanding, not shrinking, the state's capacity to surveil, police, and punish.[9] As a result of realignment, people convicted of nonserious, nonviolent, nonsexual crimes, the so-called "three nons," will serve time in county jail or be sanctioned with probation. Realignment also has done nothing to halt new jail construction taking place all over California; researchers Jacob Kang-Brown and Jack Norton demonstrate that jail construction in California shows no sign of slowing down. For example, in California's Central Valley, in 2016 and again in 2018, the state funded the expansion of King County Jail, which today rivals the jail incarceration rate of Los Angeles County.[10]

The case of criminal justice reform in California also reflects what law professor and legal scholar Hadar Aviram terms *humonetarianism* or a "set of rhetorical arguments, political strategies, correctional policies, and cultural perceptions that focuses on cost-saving and financial prudence as its *raison d'être*."[11] Aviram distinguishes six main features of criminal justice reforms during the era of "late mass incarceration," including: 1) "cost-centered discourse"; 2) rise of bipartisan coalitions; 3) sentencing reforms that focus on "low-hanging fruit" of nonviolent offenders and further drive the wedge between violent and nonviolent offenders; 4) the language of risk to categorize costly prison populations such as the elderly; 5) restructuring of carceral categories (felonies become misdemeanors, for example); and 6) shifting the burden of rehabilitation onto probationers and prisoners. As Aviram argues, the marketing of California's realignment shifted away from any language of "soft on crime" and instead focused on the financial benefits to the state, projecting savings that would be instead allocated to crime prevention programs and victim services. Aviram describes the efforts to divert nonviolent offenders while continuing to incarcerate violent offenders as the "Correctional Hunger Games," where incarcerated people are pitted against each other in a zero-sum battle.[12]

Criminal justice reform efforts in California are an example of the wider crisis of the carceral system, where older ways of thinking are being discarded and reconfigured, though not necessarily for the better. To understand the current moment, it's important to look historically at how reform movements help the system adapt to crises of legitimacy, rather than serving as steps towards its dismantling.

Carceral Crises and Legitimacy in Historical Perspective

When Michel Foucault published *Discipline and Punish* in 1975, large-scale reformatories, prisons, and asylums were undergoing a crisis of legitimacy. The rehabilitative ideal—the notion that criminals could be transformed into law-abiding citizens by the human sciences—which framed penal policy between 1930 and 1970, had been practically abandoned. Inherent in the rehabilitative ideal was a trust in criminal justice officials and the state to be a force for social good. This assumption was a holdover from the Progressive Era that was increasingly called into question by the urban rebellions and prison riots of the 1960s and '70s, and the stubborn fact that all the high-minded so-called rehabilitative programming pioneered in the decades prior did not seem to work. Many believed that the era of the prison was coming to an end. Historian David Rothman closed his book *The Discovery of the Asylum* with these optimistic words: "We have been gradually escaping from institutional responses and one can foresee the period when incarceration will be used still more rarely than it is today."[13] Three years later, Thomas Mathiesen, a Norwegian sociologist and radical prison reformer, published an incendiary text, *The Politics of Abolition*, which explored the limits radical prison reform groups were running up against in their work and called for the abolition of prisons.[14] It was in this context that Foucault's critique of the prison became a significant piece of writing.

Foucault begins *Discipline and Punish* by detailing the excruciating and very public punishment of Damiens, who had attempted but failed to kill the king of France. He then deftly juxtaposes this public execution with the excruciatingly banal timetable of prisoners' daily schedule in Mettray, a French prison colony. The contrast evocatively illustrates the shift from spectacular forms of punishment to prisons, based on the idea of locking people up to rehabilitate their minds and souls. This new form of discipline and surveillance was considered more "humane" than the spectacle of public punishment by middle-class reformers. Yet Foucault argues that this same humanitarian discourse helped to rationalize a new regime of punishment and control which extended beyond the prison into mental asylums, schools, workhouses, and factories. In short, as Foucault is eager to point out, prison reformers and prisons were born in the same moment, with the former largely responsible for producing the latter.[15]

For Foucault, the prison has been in crisis since its inception, and this hypothesis was derived in large part from the urgency of his day. As he was writing *Discipline and Punish*, rebellions in the streets and riots inside prisons called into question the role and function of the punishment system. In the u.s., they brought images of police violence to millions of Americans who previously lived in sheer ignorance, willed or not, of how much policing reinforced the racial and social order. Inside prisons, riots against inhumane conditions and racism called into question the rehabilitative ethos that progressive reformers had embraced and showed the institution of the prison to be "a race-divided and violence-ridden 'warehouse' geared solely to neutralizing social rejects by sequestering them physically from society."[16] In the famous case of Attica, New York, racism, extreme overcrowding, and brutal living conditions led prisoners to rebel. The Attica revolt was put down in a bloody blitzkrieg by then-Governor Rockefeller, a Republican who also championed "anti-crime" bills that expanded police power and created tougher penalties for drug offenses. But Attica's defiant spirit, the product of an age defined by widespread rebellion, could not be so easily eviscerated. In 1972, the New York State Special Commission on Attica, which was formed to investigate the rebellion, concluded that "the elements of replication are all around us. Attica is every prison; and every prison is Attica."[17]

A similar urgency underlies the deinstitutionalization movement that protested the carceral responses to mental health. Activists argued that confinement of people with mental health issues and trauma was inhumane. When, beginning in the 1960s, large-scale mental health asylums were closed and replaced by community-run mental health centers, anti-prison activists saw

this as an important win. But the outcome of deinstitutionalization, in the absence of broader social transformations providing
social services and support, was far from a victory for many of
those victimized by these institutions. Thousands of people were
released back into poor neighborhoods which were ill-equipped to
offer the care that activists imagined. Instead, people were shuffled
between programs, shelters, and halfway homes, living in constant poverty and despair and often committing crimes. Writing
on the heels of the deinstitutionalization movement, Andrew Scull
warned about the effects of accepting the idea that community-
based treatment was any less punitive than institutional social
control. Examining how underfunded and ill-equipped "the community" was to handle the thousands of mentally ill patients and
prisoners dumped on it, he decried decarceration as "an enterprise
[which] is built on a foundation of sand."[18] In retrospect, deinstitutionalization amounted to nothing more than the beginning
of carceral devolution, where the crisis forced a reconfiguration
in social control and punishment and the offloading of state
responsibilities to local and non-state institutions.

Scull argued that state support for deinstitutionalization and
decarceration was shaped less by a concern with improving on
the rehabilitative model than by systemic changes in capitalism,
including fiscal concerns spurred by economic difficulties. Then
as now, there were many conservatives who supported more
punitive penal policy in reaction to the failures of rehabilitative
programming to reduce the jail population or prevent the reincarceration of the same people. High rates of so-called recidiv-
ism in particular were cited to argue that education programs
inside prisons—hallmark of the rehabilitative ideal—did little
to transform prisoners into law-abiding citizens. In 1972, a
Republican congressman from Connecticut decided to spend
36 hours in prison to see conditions inside for himself. Upon his
release he told the Associated Press that prison was "a waste of
money and human life."[19]

Simultaneously, the proponents of Black and Brown Power, responding to the failure of desegregation to stamp out structural racism, turned increasingly towards demanding community control. Black radicals argued that Black institutions should operate free from the authority of white people. Applied to prisons, it was an issue on which liberals found common ground with some conservatives. Liberals argued that large-scale prisons were no longer able to rehabilitate antisocial behavior and embraced community alternatives as the answer to state institutional control and stigma. And conservatives wanted nothing more than to pass the costs of running large-scale institutions onto working-class communities. As we discussed in Chapter Two, as the 1970s wore on, the racial politics of austerity at the root of mass incarceration overwhelmed this growing consensus that prisons were good for nothing. It is no coincidence, then, that many commentators today speak of the prison buildup in the decades that followed like it was a big mistake. While this ignores the political issues at the center of mass incarceration, it is correct to say that from the vantage point of the early 1970s, the hyper-reliance on prisons that characterizes the present day was not just inevitable—it almost seemed impossible.

Accordingly, contemporary liberal reformers are driven by the desire to reduce mass incarceration to its pre-1970s levels. The main assumption is that the War on Drugs and sentencing guidelines enacted in its wake have over-criminalized and over-punished ordinary Americans in a way that runs contrary to how these institutions are *supposed to* work. This tension is also evident in Michelle Alexander's *The New Jim Crow* (2010). As important as Alexander's interventions were to popularize the ills of mass incarceration, they unfortunately reinforced the narrative that most people are locked up for small and petty nonviolent drug offenses. Counter to this widely accepted belief, drug offenders comprise only 20 percent of those in state prisons, whereas violent offenders account for twice that figure. Crucially,

Marie Gottschalk argues, even if we were to release all state prisoners charged for nonviolent drug offenses, we'd only be able to reduce incarceration by 20 percent, and the u.s. prison population would still be one of the highest in the world.[20] The focus on nonviolent low-level arrests and convictions also reaffirms the commitment of reformers to focus criminal justice reform efforts on "low-hanging fruit."

Nowhere is this commitment more visible than in the federal prison reform movement. In 2015, President Obama became the first sitting president to visit a federal correctional facility—El Reno, a federal minimum–maximum security prison outside Oklahoma City. Like many federal prisons around the country, El Reno had experienced overcrowding and escalating costs. But the choice was strategic for another reason: Oklahoma holds the top spot in the nation for the state with the highest incarceration rates, a position it often shares with Louisiana. Inside El Reno, Obama met with six prisoners, all incarcerated for nonviolent drug offenses. He remarked how common it is for young people to make mistakes—he too had smoked marijuana and tried cocaine—without noting that it was the lack of social opportunity and support that prevented these six men from thriving, much less ending up at Harvard Law School as he had. Obama's choice to meet with nonviolent offenders is representative of a larger trend in criminal justice reform today: a growing distinction between nonviolent (drug) offenses and violent offenses, the former deserving a second chance and the latter incarceration.

Throughout his two terms, Obama pardoned close to 2,000 people charged with federal crimes, many of them drug charges stemming from the mandatory "truth-in-sentencing" rules imposed in the mid-1980s, at the height of the War on Drugs. While Obama left office with a federal prison population reduced to a level not seen since the Carter Administration, focusing only on federal prison reform ignores two important factors. The first is that mass incarceration is largely a state and local phenomenon.

For example, according to the latest data, there are close to 1.3 million people held in state prisons in contrast to 226,000 in federal prisons. Secondly, due to the fact that many drug offenses fall under federal jurisdiction, federal prisons tend to incarcerate far more people convicted of drug offenses than state prisons. For instance, in 2014, while half of incarcerated people in state prisons were convicted of a violent charge, that was the case for fewer than 5 percent of the federal population.[21]

Obama's focus on nonviolent drug offenders is also emblematic of wider criminal justice reform efforts which have drawn together conservatives and liberals to reform "tough on crime" sentencing policies. In his 2004 State of the Union address, President George W. Bush proposed a prisoner rehabilitation initiative that would become the Second Chance Act in 2008. The bill authorized $165 million in federal grants to state, local, and tribal governments, and nonprofit organizations, to fund reentry programs. The bipartisan legislation sought to reform the Omnibus Crime Control and Safe Street Act of 1968 that had established the Law Enforcement Assistance Administration (LEAA) and funded local programs as part of Lyndon Johnson's "War on Crime." The bill also required federal facilities to report the use of physical restraints on female prisoners during pregnancy and childbirth.

Two years later, under the Obama administration, Congress passed the Fair Sentencing Act (originally named the Fairness in Cocaine Act), which set out to reduce the 100 to 1 disparity in the punishment for possession between crack cocaine and the same amount of powder. This disparity is widely seen in the hyper-criminalization of crack, a drug widely used by poor Black people, compared to its powder form, associated with more affluent white users. Congress's most avid supporter of the bill was, surprisingly, none other than the right-wing Alabama senator Jeff Sessions, who would go on to become attorney general under Trump. As attorney general, Sessions effectively

rolled back Obama's policy of federal restraint in drug prosecution and federal oversight of police departments, masterminded
Trump's policy of family separation at the u.s.–Mexico border,
and supported voter suppression schemes.[22] After the Fairness
in Sentencing Act went through the legislative meat grinder, the
100 to 1 disparity was reduced to 18 to 1. It was a sign of tenuous
bipartisan consensus, though one in which appearances can
be deceiving.

Austerity Makes for Strange Bedfellows: "Smart on Crime"

Perhaps no other framework better represents the collaboration
between liberals and conservatives on criminal justice reform
than that embodied in the phrase "Smart on Crime." The liberal
Washington-based think tank the Center for American Progress
has foregrounded this concept as an alternative to the tough-
versus-soft on crime debate.[23] The phrase was first popularized
by Kamala Harris, now vice president, who cut her political teeth
when, with the support of San Francisco's police unions, she beat
out her former boss and progressive district attorney Terence
Hallinan for attorney general of California. Harris published
Smart on Crime: A Career Prosecutor's Plan to Make Us Safer in
2008, expressing a vision for reforming the nation's criminal
justice system, including her preference for so-called diversion
of arrested people away from jail and prison, and alternatives to
incarceration programs more broadly. Yet as she makes clear in a
section of the book titled "Law Enforcement Not Social Work,"
drug diversion programs such as Back on Track, which Harrison
spearheaded as San Francisco's DA to keep low-level offenders
out of jail, were not developed out of "pity or compassion."[24] To
counter any critique of being "soft on crime," Harris justifies the
necessity of law enforcement to pursue low-level drug offenders
and sex workers and to prosecute parents of habitually truant
children. *Smart on Crime* is chock full of strategies to reduce

costs associated with incarceration and increase public safety by ensuring that the system remains tough on the so-called violent offenders who occupy what she calls the "top of the crime pyramid." It is a suitable text for someone who proudly proclaimed herself California's "top cop."

Since the publication of Harris's book, the Smart on Crime approach has stood for a cost-centered perspective on criminal justice reform. In 2013, Smart on Crime was adopted by Obama's State Attorney General Eric Holder as the guiding rubric for federal criminal justice reform. Holder maintained that the time had come to rethink mass incarceration and argued for a smarter approach to crime. The five principles of Smart on Crime he outlined were "prioritize prosecution of serious offenses," reform racial disparities in sentencing, encourage alternative to incarceration programs for nonviolent crimes, improve reentry, and redirect federal resources to violence prevention.[25] Three years later, the Department of Justice claimed that the reforms had worked and that there was a noticeable decline in the federal prison population due to the decision to reform federal prosecution of drug crimes.

Holder and Harris's embrace of Smart on Crime as a program of reforms aimed at low-level arrestees, in the hopes of saving criminal justice resources for more serious arrestees, is actually a page out of the Republican playbook, called Right on Crime. The latter national campaign frames mass incarceration as a fiscal problem to be fixed by shrinking government overreach and saving taxpayer money through "cost-effective" approaches to criminal justice. The Right on Crime movement was created in Texas in 2007 through a campaign by the Texas Public Policy Foundation in partnership with the American Conservative Union Foundation and Prison Fellowship. Today dozens of states including Georgia, Ohio, Kentucky, Mississippi, and Oklahoma are implementing these conservative criminal justice reforms.

One of the most active supporters of the Right on Crime movement is Newt Gingrich. In 2011, Gingrich co-wrote an op-ed in the *Washington Post* that highlighted the "urgent need to address the astronomical growth in the prison population, with its huge costs in dollars and lost human potential," calling on his fellow conservatives to "lead the way in fixing it."[26] Since then, Gingrich has continuously voiced his support for criminal justice reform. He even appeared in Ava DuVernay's 2016 film *13th*, voicing his critique of drug policies that punished crack users disproportionately simply for being Black and poor. In 2016, in a guest column for the Louisiana-based newspaper *The Advocate*, Gingrich and his fellow conservative Pat Nolan argued against locking up juveniles in adult prisons, stating that "jails and prisons are the graduate schools of crime."[27]

The conservative push for criminal justice reform came to a head in Texas, which is known to have one of the harshest penal systems in the country, and where Republicans have long prided themselves on being "tough on crime." Governor Rick Perry was once quoted as saying, "If you come into our state and you kill one of our children, you kill a police officer, you're involved with another crime and you kill one of our citizens, you will face the ultimate justice in the state of Texas, and that is, you will be executed."[28] Within the span of five years, Texas built 38 prisons and saw its correctional spending nearly double from $1.4 to $2.4 billion by the 2000s. Even though some may see this as an exorbitant amount, it was still "just 3 or 4 percent of the total state budget, or roughly what it spends on highways each year."[29] For decades, conservatives have promoted privatization schemes to keep incarceration costs low. By 2007, Texas prisons were facing a crisis of overcrowding and officials feared they would not have enough prison beds. In response to this crisis, the Texas Public Policy Foundation (TPPF) launched the Right on Crime campaign, which advocates "conservative solutions for reducing crime, restoring victims, reforming offenders, and lowering taxpayer costs."[30] TPPF and Right on Crime conducted research which demonstrated that the state would have to spend $2 billion in new prison construction to accommodate projections that the state would need 17,000 new beds by 2012. They argued against the proposal and instead pushed for cheaper alternatives. In response to this pressure, lawmakers ended up defeating the proposal to construct new prisons and instead expanded probation and parole, along with substance and mental health treatment, to divert people to community supervision.

The Texas case was widely seen as a win for the Right on Crime coalition. Overnight the state was transformed into a model for national criminal justice reform, even receiving accolades from well-established liberal organizations such as the ACLU. In its report of 2011, "Smart Reform Is Possible," the ACLU praised Texas as an example of how states can reduce incarceration and corrections budgets while upholding the sanctity of public safety.[31] Since 2007, thirty states have followed Texas's lead and reduced lengthy prison sentences, strengthened diversion and alternatives to incarceration programs, and eliminated mandatory minimum sentencing. But reforms in Texas and elsewhere have not been the magic bullet that conservatives and liberals have claimed they are.

Instead, as Marie Gottschalk argues, the Texan model has emerged as a way to run mass incarceration "on the cheap."[32] Gottschalk shows that the eagerness of conservatives and their allies to lend legitimacy to their "smart on crime" efforts relied on "a selective reading" of incarceration figures which does not take into account the new prison beds that have been built to house parole violators and those undergoing substance abuse treatment. Further, as has been the case nationally, powerful organizations like the bail industry and police unions have opposed various reform efforts. Above all, the adoption of alternatives means to surveil and confine people in the community, such as electronic monitoring, house arrest, and routine drug testing—all of which have been pushed by private contractors—have been embraced by states and counties seeking to save money while continuing to maintain a punishment regime. On paper, the people caught in these coercive systems can be celebrated as freed from jail and prison. But they have not been freed from the meshes of the system, and remain very much in thrall to a punishment apparatus that surveils and limits their mobility, at best, and at worst leads right back behind bars.

Looking at state expenditures on corrections, a key talking point that has united conservatives and liberals, Gottschalk notes a paradox: while, since the 1970s, so-called corrections as a share of state expenditures have risen second to Medicaid, they nonetheless remain a small percentage of overall state budgets. For example, while corrections budgets oscillated between 2 and 3 percent of state budgets between 1982 and 2010, state spending on education was between 29 and 33 percent and public welfare between 22 and 25 percent.[33] This has, however, not stopped many state lawmakers and reformers from adopting the language of fiscal concerns to push for reforms. Yet, as Gottschalk and other scholars such as Hadar Aviram, Ruth Wilson Gilmore, Christopher Seeds, and Sarah Cate have emphasized, the fiscal argument has done very little to end mass incarceration and instead has led to a reconfigured carceral state that continues to skim at the top: namely, by recalibrating the sentencing of nonviolent offenders and continuing its commitment to locking up and punishing violent offenders.[34]

Perhaps no piece of legislation is more emblematic of these pitfalls than the passage of the First Step Act, which drew praise from conservatives and liberals alike. The act was part of a strange political moment when President Trump, who had run on a platform of "law and order," undertook notable reforms to the punishment system. Even as he undid Obama-era reforms of policing, Trump signed this law aimed at reforming federal prisons and sentencing guidelines, notably shortening mandatory minimums for nonviolent drug offenders, easing "three strike" laws, restricting the use of restraints on pregnant women, mandating so-called de-escalation training for corrections staff, and increasing "good conduct time" credits from 47 to 54 days per year.[35] The bill was cosponsored by Vice President Mike Pence, White House senior advisor Jared Kushner and Democratic New Jersey Senator Cory Booker. It was even endorsed by the Fraternal Order of Police. The legislation released certain federal prisoners, based on a complex eligibility calculus, which, as Gottschalk argues, does very little to reform sentencing guidelines, since the vast majority of those incarcerated are in state and county facilities, not federal prisons.[36]

In short, despite the rosy rhetoric surrounding it, the First Step Act should not be confused with a move away from hyper-punitive politics in Washington, DC. The centerpiece of the act was the adoption of risk-assessment tools that heavily weighted defendants' criminal histories to calculate whether they are eligible for release. Risk-assessment tools are widespread across all carceral institutions today. In the previous chapter, we examined how risk-assessment tools reinforce race- and class-based inequalities and are popular attempts to privatize and offload the responsibility to punish from the state to third-party organizations. In this instance, we see risk assessment also being used to further drive the distinction between violent and non-violent offenders, the latter seen as the only one worth saving from the clutches of the carceral state. The reliance on risk-assessment tools or algorithms to predict future criminal behavior also dovetails with liberal commitments to using data and technology to create a *smaller, safer, and fairer* system of justice. The result is not a lessening of punishment, however, but simply a transformation of the carceral state at a time when the politics of cutting public expenditures no matter what has finally come to prisons.

The New York Decarceration Miracle

New York is another key example of the pitfalls of criminal justice reform. The state has been hailed by liberals as a case in point of successful decarceration. Yet a closer look at the constellation of forces that have pushed for the closure of Rikers Island and bail reform reveals a landscape of decarceration that will likely follow suit in other cities. In New York, since the late 1990s, incarceration rates have declined by a quarter, the reform and repeal of Rockefeller Drug Laws have released thousands of low-hanging fruit (namely, nonviolent drug cases), and twelve juvenile facilities have been closed. Initiatives such as Close to Home have transferred remaining youth to the supervision of local nonprofits and city agencies. Pressure by local activists has ended stop-and-frisk, jail populations have significantly dropped, and pre-trial diversion—an alternative to prosecution programs which has diverted only qualifying first-time defendants from serving jail time—and bail supervision alternatives have been piloted and adopted by nonprofit organizations.

Despite small decarceration efforts, incarceration costs continued to skyrocket. In 2013, the city's Independent Budget Office released statistics that noted the city spent $167,000 annually incarcerating people on Rikers Island. One reporter wryly commented that these costs made Rikers Island jail cells more expensive than any apartment in Chelsea or the West Village.[37] All the while, continuous scandal engulfed the island penal colony, perhaps especially the case of Kalief Browder. His three-year ordeal in city custody called attention to the potentially disastrous effects of probation, bail, and other practices conceived as alternatives to incarceration under New York City's present punishment regime, which ended up instead keeping Browder locked on Rikers Island for over three years. But it also raised the call for the island's carceral facilities to be shuttered once and for all.[38]

In response to Browder's case—and, ultimately, his untimely death by suicide—abolitionists raised the call: shut down Rikers.[39] The city's carceral nonprofits crafted a counteroffer. Between 2016 and 2017, one of the city's progressive judges led a cohort of criminal justice reformers to study how to reduce the jail population of Rikers Island. Their final report, *A More Just City*, called for the downsizing of the city jail system through bail reform and alternatives to incarceration programs and relocating the remaining small number of prisoners to new state-of-the-art borough-wide jails. The commission saw this plan as an opportunity to address the legitimacy crisis facing the city's correctional institutions, and recommended neighborhood-based jails as a way of further integrating criminal justice institutions into the so-called community. The slickly designed jails, or what the commission euphemistically dubbed "justice hubs," would serve as a mixed-used space for incarcerating working-class New Yorkers, while providing yuppies with space for yoga studios and cafés on the ground level.[40] This plan drew on designs pioneered by former DOC commissioner Martin Horn, which were defeated a decade prior amid fierce community opposition, including from abolitionists.[41] This time around, however, the advocates of a sweeping $10 billion jail construction plan could count on the support of a whole nexus of criminal justice reform nonprofits affiliated with the Ford Foundation, which deployed the language of social justice, and even abolition, to advocate for the erection of skyscraper jails across New York City. To date, despite a valiant abolitionist opposition under the banner of "No New Jails," this juggernaut plan is moving forward, as New York City prepares to significantly expand its jail capacity, with no binding commitment to even close Rikers.

Carceral Nonprofits and Recuperation

New York City has long been a laboratory of carceral reform efforts, and this most recent plan to integrate jails and other criminal justice institutions into the community is an important bellwether of the kinds of reforms that we will continue to see. The fight to close Rikers Island also reveals how much the political terrain of mass incarceration has shifted. Few elites, save for perhaps the correctional union brass, would publicly argue to keep Rikers Island as is, and many have moved toward advocating for its closure, but with the catch of replacing it with "nicer" jails. This case demonstrates how progressive political emissaries of the ruling class are willing to downsize and even close some prisons and jails, paying great lip service to America's legacy of racism, and making other symbolic gestures toward the demands of mass movement—all in order to maintain the public's faith in the legitimacy of the capitalist system, and build a more efficient system of punishment and control.

One of the most significant transformations of the last decades, visible in New York and in the similar struggles against jail closures in Los Angeles and Atlanta, is the growth of a powerful nonprofit sector which increasingly shares with the state the responsibilities of managing urban poverty. While the hard right intransigently opposes mass movements, the most far-sighted among the ruling class recognizes them as opportunities to stabilize capital accumulation and incorporate the dynamism of working-class movements into sustained ruling-class domination. In moments of crisis, these foundations and nonprofits become indispensable for recuperating radical demands like decarceration, towards innovating new forms of social control. It is a model pioneered by the Ford Foundation, which financially supported many of the community control efforts launched by various organizations during the Black Power era, successfully channeling anger at the white supremacist system toward reforms that shifted the burden of providing social services to communities of color. Since the 1970s, as America's system of mass incarceration has ossified, the role of this third-party sector has become even more important. Today it doesn't just compensate for the state's unwillingness to care for the poor but serves as a research and development arm guiding the state's punishment policy, while fighting to rescue the legitimacy of the punishment system from a growing chorus of critics.

These "carceral nonprofits," as we term them, have emerged as powerful players advocating for a more humane system of mass incarceration, like smaller neighborhood jails. Simultaneously, they have promoted widespread punishment and control, even jockeying on behalf of the nonprofit sector for a cut of the action designing carceral facilities and administering punishment.[42] As a humanist critique of mass incarceration permeates the mainstream, the casting of jails and prisons as places where people can obtain help and services, a discourse James Kilgore refers to as "carceral humanism," is gaining traction in response.[43] When New York City debated its jail expansion plan, this mantle was even adopted by the putative abolitionist Soffiyah Elijah, who argued that opposing these jails was tantamount to opposing the social services the city claimed they would provide.[44] The irony of course is that someone has to be arrested and jailed in order to receive any kind of social services. In recent years, Elijah's words point to a trend well underway, as jails around the nation are increasingly moving to rebrand jails as mental health facilities.

For example, in Los Angeles, which has one of the largest jail populations in the nation, the LA County Board of Supervisors approved a $2.2-billion plan in 2016 to replace the old and dilapidated Men's Central Jail with a "mental health treatment center," as a part of the county's embrace of a "care first, jail last" ethics.[45] However, an even more controversial part of the plan included relocating the women's jail from southeast LA to an Immigration and Customs Enforcement (ICE) center about 80 miles away from the city. A group of dedicated abolitionists came together in coalitions with other grassroots organizations under the banner JusticeLA, fought against the plan, and ultimately succeeded in defeating it.[46]

Abolitionist fights in New York City and Los Angeles reveal a shifting terrain in punishment, as urban cities in particular move to replace costly incarceration with so-called alternatives to incarceration, which turn the world outside prison into a complex forcefield of surveillance and control. These programs cannot be seriously called alternatives to incarceration, since their punitive and unforgiving nature often makes them precursors to it.[47] Decarceration, as abolitionist scholar Brendan McQuade argues, realigns perfectly with the principles of mass supervision, which emphasizes managing and controlling poor people within the community, namely through "carceral nonprofits" and other forms of private–public partnerships, like community policing.[48]

Taken in sum, decentralization of carceral institutions, the expansion of alternatives to incarceration and diversion programs, and the devolution of so-called rehabilitation to community-based organizations ends up being a lot cheaper than a jail or prison cell. These practices also maintain and reinforce the distinction between violent and nonviolent offenders that has been central to contemporary criminal justice reforms. Diversion programs supervise nonviolent offenders on the outside, while costly incarceration in jails and prisons is reserved for violent criminals. *Voilà*: mass incarceration is scaled back, made more humane, and more cost-effective. In this way, decarceration and criminal justice reforms have become an exercise in borrowing from Peter to pay Paul.

For example, while reformers remain optimistic about decarceration efforts in New York City, Chicago, and Los Angeles, where jail populations have seen some significant reductions, the opposite is true of rural America. Since 2013, jail incarceration in rural counties has increased by 27 percent while urban incarceration has declined by 18 percent.[49] Another study found that rates of pre-trial jail detention in rural counties have increased by 436 percent between 1970 and 2013.[50] This can be explained by the increased poverty of rural residents, lack of pre-trial detention diversion programs, and also the ways in which local county officials rent beds to hold people from state, federal, and immigrant detention facilities. The rising rural jail population doesn't neatly fit into the narrative of mass incarceration which emphasizes urban policies. In rural areas we see a similar constellation of forces to punish the poor, but often with much less oversight and scrutiny.

Even with all the money thrown at the problem, reforming the American carceral state has proven difficult. Contrary to what many liberals think, this is not due to lack of political willpower. In the present moment, both parties have expressed sincere commitment to reforming America's punishment regime, which can be confusing to many activists. But as we have argued, there are larger structural forces that cannot simply be reformed through legislation: namely, the turbulent and deepening contradictions of a class society that is being governed from one disaster to the next. As the crisis of the carceral state deepens, radicals and abolitionists risk being drawn by liberal and conservative forces into managing the growing contradictions of American capitalist society, under the auspices of humanism and decarceration. In the next chapter we analyze the promise and potential pitfalls of abolitionism as it exists within this unique historical juncture.

five

"Defund the Police": At the Crossroads of Revolution and Reform

In early June 2020, Washington, DC, Mayor Muriel E. Bowser ordered "Black Lives Matter" painted in bold yellow in the street alongside an entire city block near the White House. If it was a move designed to placate protesters and provoke President Trump, it only succeeded in the latter. The following day, rebels decided to add their own messaging: "Defund the Police."[1] As the fires of Minneapolis still smoldered, calls to defund police departments quickly came to define the horizon for the rebellion. The political forces advancing this demand were multifarious, including national politicians such as Representative Alexandria Ocasio-Cortez, alongside putative anarchists and socialists, and many young people coming to left politics for the first time. Surely some of this exemplified Marx and Engels's observation that "part of the bourgeoisie is desirous of redressing social grievances, in order to secure the continued existence of bourgeois society."[2] Nonetheless, the Defund movement drew its theoretical and organizational impetus from the longstanding U.S. political tradition of abolitionism, which envisions a society where violent compulsion is no longer a central feature of social life. This tradition became the dominant political paradigm with which the rebels of 2020 have made sense of their activity and mapped the political terrain ahead. It therefore requires serious critical engagement.

"As a society, we have been so indoctrinated with the idea that we solve problems by policing and caging people that many cannot imagine anything other than prisons and the police as solutions to violence and harm," abolitionist activist-scholar Mariame Kaba wrote in a provocative *New York Times* op-ed of 2020 entitled "Yes, We Mean Literally Abolish the Police." Kaba continued: "People like me who want to abolish prisons and police, however, have a vision of a different society, built on cooperation instead of individualism, on mutual aid instead of self-preservation."[3] The primary focus of Kaba's work is on cultivating alternative methods of addressing conflict and harm within our present society that do not revolve around the coercive appendages of the state. Survived & Punished, the organization Kaba helped to cofound, is a direct outgrowth of organizing by feminists of color to support survivors of sexual violence who have been criminalized for defending themselves. And like many abolitionists, Kaba is clear the project must have the end of capitalism as its ultimate aim. "You're not going to be able to end policing without ending capitalism," she recently argued, "abolition has to be an internationalist project, as well as an anti-capitalist project, as well as a project that is rooted in constantly thinking about concentrated violence across the board."[4]

As the carceral state became a political issue in the minds of millions of Americans, the abolitionist worldview has provided a set of analytic and organizational tools for the project of human emancipation.

The strengths of abolitionism are also its weaknesses; the emphasis abolitionists place on practical activity in the here and now has led to an underdeveloped conception of what a revolutionary transformation of society along abolitionist lines would actually look like. Can it be done utilizing the framework of the existing state? Can it be accomplished peacefully? Or will it require an extra-legal, and likely violent, confrontation with the ruling class and its loyalists? Should abolitionists invest their energy in the progressive wing of the state to one day take it over, or is the state itself an enemy, Ocasio-Cortez and all? These are not abstract questions, since they inform how we engage concretely in the present. While abolitionists acknowledge that interpersonal harm and conflict cannot be divorced from state violence, the present impetus of abolitionist organizing remains focused on transforming personal relations and building communal alternatives to repressive agencies of the state. Are these organizations part of an organized revolutionary offensive, or efforts to live comfortably on the margins of an otherwise capitalist society? Should we expect these community-building projects to scale up, replacing the existing society? What would this process look like? The exact relationship between abolition and revolution has not been sufficiently developed. While abolitionism aims at a future society defined by human needs, and not exploitation, the nature of this society—and how we can get there from the present—remains under-theorized.

In this chapter we return to the political topography of the post-rebellion moment, when the demand to "defund the police" emerged as a popular rallying cry in response to racist police violence, and moved a hitherto marginal political discourse about downsizing or outright abolishing the carceral state into the mainstream. We discuss the profundity of this demand, its radical potential, and the risks of its co-optation into the dead end of reform for its own sake. To this effect, we pay particular attention to the abolitionist strategy of "non-reformist reforms," the idea that fighting for objectives such as fewer jails and diminished police budgets can lead toward social revolution, not simply toward reforms as ends in themselves.

The u.s. Abolitionist Tradition

On June 9, 1972, Angela Davis, newly released from jail after
serving sixteen months for her alleged involvement in Jonathan
Jackson's armed takeover of a California courtroom, addressed
a multiracial crowd of 1,500 supporters gathered at the Embassy
Auditorium in Los Angeles:

> We must be about the business of building a movement so
> strong and so powerful that it will not only free individuals
> like me—like the Soledad Brothers, the San Quentin Six, Billy
> Dean Smith—but one which will begin to attack the very
> foundations of the prison system itself.
>
> And in doing this, the prison movement must be
> integrated into our struggles for Black and Brown liberation,
> and to our struggles for an end to material want and need.
> A very long struggle awaits us. And we know that it would be
> very romantic and idealistic to entertain immediate goals of
> tearing down all the walls of all the jails and prisons through-
> out this country. We should take on the task of freeing as
> many of our sisters and brothers as possible. And at the
> same time, we must demand the ultimate abolition of the
> prison system along with the revolutionary transformation
> of this society.[5]

In her speech, Davis reinforced the relationship that Black
radicals have often asserted between liberation struggles and
anti-police and prison movements, none more so than Black
Panther activists in the 1960s and '70s. In 1966, the Black Panther
Party (BPP) was founded in Oakland, California, to monitor
police activities in poor Black neighborhoods. In their Ten Point
Program, "What We Want Now," the BPP called for an end to
police brutality and murder of Black people and freedom for all
those incarcerated in jails and prisons.

By the 1970s, the state crackdown on the BPP led to the incarceration of many of its members, who all of a sudden found themselves in cells with other poor and working-class Black men and women. Panther members took the opportunity to build relationships with other incarcerated people to fight against prison conditions. For example, Albert Woodfox and Herbert Wallace organized Black prisoners against rape and sexual assault through the newly established Black Panther Chapter inside Angola, the infamous maximum-security prison in Louisiana, built on a former cotton plantation and named after an African territory from which white planters had bought slaves.[6] In October 1970, prison revolts in five detention facilities in New York City, including the Tombs and Rikers Island, were influenced by members of the BPP and the Young Lords, a Puerto Rican organization formed in emulation of the BPP.[7] In 1971 Black radical George Jackson, a former BPP member, was shot and killed inside San Quentin prison. Two weeks later, in reaction to his death and the conditions inside the New York State prison Attica, the institution erupted in a riot. The political context of Black Power and the connections that revolutionaries drew between life on the inside and outside of prison walls was important for the organizing work that Black feminists took up to challenge the carceral state.

Anti-Carceral Feminism

The Panthers and their fellow travelers were organizing against the double-edged sword of racist austerity: on the one hand, the state was investing its repressive capacities in keeping working-class people of color in their place, while on the other it was withdrawing public spending from the communities that needed it the most. The figure of state abandonment which characterized the Panthers' service programs, like the free breakfast initiative, was part of a broader movement among Black radicals to make up for this calculated neglect. Beth Richie, a long-time Black feminist and activist, recounts that since at least the 1970s organizers against domestic violence and sexual assault had a difficult time getting the issues taken seriously by the state. When police and courts finally got tough on these issues, the result was more criminalization and incarceration, instead of resources for the survivors of violence. Police and court involvement, Richie argues, only creates further chaos and instability in communities where violence is the product of a lack of material resources and community self-determination.[8] In contrast to the punitive approach to interpersonal violence, abolitionists like Richie argue that a primary task of organizing is to build up these communal capacities, coupled with the withdrawal of policing and incarceration, to a sufficient level for communities to handle antisocial behavior independently of the carceral state. This means eliminating the presence of police, courts, and jails in communities, while simultaneously strengthening communal responses to violence and other forms of antisocial behavior when they arise. While it is a common line among dismissive critics today that abolitionists are naive idealists, especially around the question of violence, the genesis of much of today's abolitionism can be traced directly back to practical engagements with the reality of interpersonal violence, and the failure of the carceral approach to make things any better.

As Emily L. Thuma chronicles in *All Our Trials: Prisons, Policing, and the Feminist Fight to End Violence*, the growth of the carceral state in the 1970s and '80s not only produced repression against revolutionaries but "created new political opportunities for the feminist anti-rape and battered women's movement."[9] In the 1970s, a series of criminal defense trials where Black, Latinx, and indigenous women faced serious prison time for killing their assailant in self-defense helped to solidify Black feminist commitment to fighting state violence inside prison walls. Of particular importance was the case of Joan Little in 1974, which the *Chicago Tribune* dubbed the "trial of the century," involving a twenty-year-old incarcerated Black woman who murdered a white guard to protect herself from rape. As Angela Davis pointed out in her staunch defense of Joan Little in a 1975 issue of *Ms.* magazine, the case made evident the sexual exploitation that Black women endured in American society. "Race and male supremacy," Davis argued, "have to be projected in their dialectical unity. In the case of the raped black woman, they are mutually reinforcive."[10] The Joan Little case helped bolster a multiracial movement led by Black feminists that also drew in white revolutionary feminists, and that indicted the prison industrial complex and pointed to the need for antiracist organizing against state violence.

As Thuma lays out, the court victories of Joan Little and other similar cases involving indigenous and Latinx women pushed feminists to take up seriously the issues facing incarcerated women of color. Feminists established prison support collectives to challenge mainstream ideas about prisons and published radical newsletters that drew attention to issues facing incarcerated women, often using explicit abolitionist language. These newsletters became an important way for incarcerated women to connect with each other and those on the outside and strategize against violence in prisons which often included forced drugging, shackling during childbirth, sexual assault, rape, and forced sterilizations. One example of such abolitionist-inspired prison support collectives Thuma focuses on is Women Free Women in Prison (WFWP), a primarily white working-class and lesbian group which in 1974 came together to organize support for incarcerated women at Bedford Hills prison in upstate New York, who were involved in a rebellion against prison conditions, including the beating of a Black woman named Carol Crooks.[11] The "August Rebellion" at Bedford Hills was met with repression by prison authorities that transferred Crooks and other women involved in the uprising to the Matteawan State Hospital for the Criminally Insane in Dutchess County. As Thuma recounts, the WFWP organized car rides to visit the women incarcerated there and organized coalitions to defend women at Bedford Hills who decided to go on strike four years later in 1978.

The 1970s and '80s also saw feminist organizing for the establishment of rape crisis centers structured around the principles of mutual aid. The DC Rape Crisis Center, run by and for women of color, was a prime example of the new institutions that feminists sought to create in the 1970s. However, outside of a revolutionary movement context, as Thuma argues, some of these centers became beholden to funders and to criminal justice agencies and lost the autonomy on which they were founded. As feminists fought for autonomous institutions that would address violence outside of the punishment system, spending on policing and prisons reached unprecedented levels. The Law Enforcement Assistance Administration (LEAA) became a major player in the federal government, pouring millions of dollars into crime-control programs and policies. A new generation of conservative criminologists attempted to capture the ideological terrain and advocate for a more punitive response to the rise in unemployment and crime of the 1970s, shifting the debate to the right.

In response to the growing threat of Black radicalism and right-wing law-and-order politics, liberal nonprofits emerged. In April 1972, the National Council on Crime and Delinquency (NCCD) issued a policy statement that called for a halt to construction of all prisons, jails, juvenile training schools, and detention homes until all other alternatives to incarceration had been exhausted. The following year the National Advisory Commission on Criminal Justice Standards and Goals also recommended a ten-year moratorium on prison construction and a phasing out of large-scale institutions. In Massachusetts, in an unprecedented move, Jerome Miller, the director of Massachusetts Department of Youth Services (DYS), closed all of the juvenile prisons and detention centers and transferred remaining youth to community-based alternative programs. In 1975, the National Moratorium on Prison Construction was established in Washington, DC, and advocated for employment as an alternative to incarceration. But law-and-order intellectuals and ideologues were successful in portraying penal abolition, and even reform, as unrealistic utopian demands in the face of increasing crime and disorder, as the phenomenon we today know as mass incarceration kicked into high gear.

By the 1980s, activists organizing against the booming prison system and a general rightward shift in U.S. society were largely shoveling against the tide, however valiantly. But resistance to policing and prisons at a grassroots level did not completely dissipate. For example, the early 1990s saw the growth of groups invested in reform efforts, such as Families Against Mandatory Minimums, founded in 1991 to challenge mandatory sentencing laws and advocate for criminal justice reform. The prison moratorium efforts of the 1970s were revived once again. In 1995 Brooklyn activists established the Prison Moratorium Project, emerging as key players in the Justice 4 Youth Coalition, which in 2002 successfully stopped the city from building new youth jails (at a projected cost of $64.2 million).[12] The same year, on the West Coast, the California Prison Moratorium Project was created with the explicit goal of halting new prison construction. But these efforts were largely localized and unable to counteract the onslaught of the carceral state at the most intense period of its growth.

At this time, working-class Black America was reeling from decades of Reganomics and right-wing politics, which had stagnated and even reversed legal and material gains supposedly won in the 1960s. In 1992, riots spread throughout Los Angeles in reaction to the exoneration of the five cops who viciously beat Rodney King in a protracted ordeal caught on videotape and publicized widely. That same year, Bill Clinton was elected president on a "tough on crime" platform designed to beat the Republicans at their own game. As president, he paired this punitive vision with crushing austerity, making good on his promise to "end welfare as we know it." This "new" Democratic Party would do everything it could to distance itself from the social spending that characterized the party from the New Deal through the Great Society, except when that spending was on military, policing, or prison infrastructure. The Omnibus Crime Bill of 1994 cemented the shift of public-spending priorities—now a bipartisan consensus—away from so-called welfare and toward the buildup of the largest prison system the world has ever known. This bill was followed a few years later with the passage of the Personal Rights and Responsibility and Work Act, which almost completely destroyed what little safety net remained for poor Americans.

The U.S. left in this period existed as small groups, mostly in Black nationalist circles in cities with histories of hot struggle, or small ideological grouplets concentrated around universities, centered on such issues as affirmative action, support for political prisoners including Mumia Abu-Jamal, and resistance to the New York Rockefeller Drug Laws. The 1990s also saw the rise of small anarchist networks such as the federation Love and Rage, which built on the anti-authoritarian ethos of the New Left to articulate a vision for anti-capitalist revolution distinct from the top-down revolutionary parties that increasingly seemed like historical relics. Revolutionaries like Noel Ignatiev, John Garvey, Beth Henson, Joel Olson, and others writing in the journal *Race Traitor*, advocated a distinctly American approach to revolution modeled after the nineteenth-century abolitionists. In 1995, Nation of Islam Leader Louis Farrakhan led the Million Man March on Washington, signaling the enduring legacy of Black nationalism dating back decades, albeit in an increasingly reactionary form. Issue-based campaigns around women's and gay rights continued within large cities, though with a decidedly liberal bent, bespeaking most coalitions' control by middle-class strivers to success under capitalism. The decade ended with the Battle of Seattle, part of a series of direct-action protests against the hothouse restructuring of global production and circulation, to the great detriment of working-class people, taking place under the short-hand of "globalization." A patriotic fever dream following the 9/11 attacks, and the subsequent "War on Terror," took the wind out of this movement's sails, setting the stage for a doomed anti-war movement and a time of great confusion and disorientation among the friends of human liberation operating in the United States. This was the political context in which the contemporary form of u.s. abolitionism took shape.

Critical Resistance

In September 1998, a network of abolitionist organizers hosted the conference "Critical Resistance: Beyond the Prison Industrial Complex" in Berkeley, California. The conference brought together 3,500 people, including anti-prison activists, academics, and formerly incarcerated people. The gathering of disparate tendencies of abolitionism and a variety of actors in one place had an energizing effect on the national movement. The group of people who had organized the conference became the collective Critical Resistance (CR). The conference, and the momentum that it generated in the coming years in left circles, brought together activists involved in campaigns against prison expansion, inhumane prison conditions, the death penalty, immigration detention, and policing, alongside activists supporting political prisoners, fighting for indigenous self-determination, and opposing u.s. imperialism. The sheer breadth of issues under the purview of CR is attested by the topics discussed in a special issue of the journal Social Justice, published in 2000 under the heading "Critical Resistance to the Prison-Industrial Complex."

The label "prison industrial complex" (PIC), first used by historian Mike Davis and subsequently popularized by Eric Schlosser and Angela Davis, allowed CR to conceptualize a broad-based movement that looked at prison expansion and conditions, but also at the multifarious social institutions that comprise the carceral state, including policing in schools, immigration enforcement, and the disciplinary coercion built into the receipt of public assistance, especially after the Clinton era.[13] The nexus of scholars and activists around CR helped craft a nuanced theory for understanding these seemingly disparate trends as part of a totality.

Much of the theoretical heft for this new movement of abolitionists was provided by founding member Angela Davis, a veteran of the Black Power movement and the Communist Party. Active in the abolitionist movement of the 1970s, Davis imbued that movement with a historical understanding of the U.S. struggle, emphasizing continuity between chattel slavery and imprisonment in the late twentieth century. In particular, Davis drew on W.E.B. Du Bois' *Black Reconstruction in America* to task abolitionist organizing with completing the work of the "abolitionist democracy" begun with Reconstruction, which for Davis offers a model for radical egalitarian democracy.[14] CR was also lent a sophisticated Marxist lens by scholar Ruth Wilson Gilmore, whose analyzed the California prison system as the racialized management of surplus populations amid capitalist crisis, not simply the consequence of ideological racism, the continuation of slavery, or the use of prisoner labor for profit, as popular activist accounts typically argue.[15]

CR became a hub of abolitionist campaigns, working closely in coalitions with groups such as the California Prison Moratorium Project and Californians United for a Responsible Budget (CURB) to fight criminalization of working-class communities of color, and stop the creation of new prison infrastructure. In 2001, a coalition of groups including CR and the Moratorium Project temporarily halted a maximum-security prison in California, building an opposition strong enough to discourage more prison-building. CURB alone estimates its activity has defeated prison expansion to the tune of 140,000 beds since 2004. This national network of abolitionists was instrumental in campaigns that stopped the construction of a jail in the Bronx, New York, in 2009. In Oakland, abolitionists kicked the Urban Shield SWAT weapons expo, a pipeline of militarized police technology, out of the city in 2014, and in 2017 made Oakland the first city to forswear the use of gang injunctions that create heightened legal penalties against accused gang members. This work was also lent impetus by the "War on Terror": in discussing U.S. imperialism along with mass incarceration and the militarization of U.S. borders, abolitionists crafted an internationalist approach to abolitionism that understood the violence of the state at home and abroad as linked to the domination at the core of capitalist society.[16]

Despite CR's abolitionist campaigns, challenges to the punishment system were increasingly mired in reforms and occurred largely within the context of nonprofit organizations that limited what could be achieved. In 2000, in response to the ways in which mainstream social service organizations had undermined the radical and abolitionist roots of the antiviolence movement, various activists working on issues related to social justice and domestic violence convened in Santa Cruz, California. The gathering, "The Color of Violence Conference on Violence Against Women of Color," represented decades of abolitionist organizing, specifically around pervasive violence against women and the failure of the state to do anything but make it worse. Angela Davis was the keynote speaker, and the event was a huge success—2,000 people were turned away due to lack of space.[17]

Buoyed by the remarkable interest their conference generated, organizers decided to continue their work through a new national network, INCITE! Women of Color Against Violence. INCITE! collaborated closely with Critical Resistance and continued to build on decades of Black feminist organizing against domestic violence. They developed a distinctly abolitionist practice based on two related issues: on the one hand, interpersonal violence is a persistent fact of American society, and, on the other, the use of police and prisons to respond to violence has not made the situation any better, especially in the working-class communities of color already hit hardest by underdevelopment and police violence. This work strives to cultivate an approach to handling antisocial behavior that does not rely on the coercive agents of the state or expand the power these agents have in working-class life, but that simultaneously does not, as do many on the left, downplay the reality of violence and antisocial behavior that permeates U.S. society. In 2015, INCITE! held their fifteenth anniversary conference in Chicago, during which they established a new national coalition, Survived & Punished, dedicated to organizing campaigns similar to those waged in defense of Joan Little in the 1970s.

Today, as the U.S. police come under scrutiny the likes of which they haven't seen in decades and mount a spirited defense in the form of Blue Lives Matter and other right-wing campaigns, it is helpful to recall the argument of Kaba, Richie, and others that the police response to violence has not actually engendered safety in any meaningful sense. By contrast, abolitionists argue that safety comes from social arrangements where everyone has everything they need to live comfortably, and conflicts are resolved on the communal level and not through the punishment system. Much of the abolitionist activity in the present involves experiments in restorative and transformative justice, and practices of mediation that resolve conflicts and attempt to address the consequences of antisocial behavior without cops or prisons.

Recalling important abolitionist work from the 1970s, CR has republished the guide *Instead of Prisons: A Handbook for Abolitionists*, originally put out by the Prison Research Education Action Project in 1976, which furnished a host of helpful alternatives to reliance on the carceral state for negotiating fraught social dynamics and responding to antisocial behavior.[18] Updating this theory for the present terrain, the collective INCITE! produced the valuable anthology *The Revolution Will Not Be Funded*, critically appraising the nonprofit organizations forming what they dubbed "the nonprofit industrial complex."[19] This work provided a new generation of activists with a vocabulary for critically assessing the nonprofit organizations that had proliferated throughout u.s. society, particularly amid state disinvestment from reproducing working-class life. The anthology observes that these organizations often adopt the rhetoric of abolitionism and anti-capitalism, hire radicals from communities of color, and foreground them in the organization's public image. All the while, these nonprofits' actual practices tend to stick to their social role of mediating class conflict and reproducing the lowest tiers of the working class, all the while, as nonprofits, helping the millionaires and billionaires who fund them shield their assets from taxation. The theory produced by INCITE! and others in understanding these organizations is vital for mapping the present terrain, especially as it relates to the thorny issue of campaigning for reforms.

Non-Reformist Reforms

Central to most abolitionist campaigns is the concept of non-reformist reforms. In a recent essay, abolitionists Dan Berger, Mariame Kaba, and David Stein define such reforms as "measures that reduce the power of an oppressive system while illuminating the system's inability to solve the crises it creates."[20] Since its formulation by the New Left revolutionary André Gorz, and subsequent popularization by abolitionists like Ruth Wilson Gilmore, the concept of non-reformist reform has come to mean different things to different organizers. For contemporary abolitionists, the basic criterion for non-reformist reforms is that they must *not* strengthen the power, social scope, and funding base of the carceral state. Abolitionists argue that additional funding, capacity, and, perhaps worst of all, legitimacy for punishment institutions will not lessen the brutality of the carceral state, but effectively expand and deepen its power. Preventing the construction of a single prison will not abolish the carceral state, of course, but it can have the effect of stemming the expansion of the state's carceral capacity, while building up a movement against the punishment system. Ultimately, non-reformist reforms scrutinize whether a demand will weaken carceral apparatuses, not its direct relationship to waging revolution.

A clear example of the non-reformist reform criterion in use comes to us from the struggle over closing Rikers Island. The death of Kalief Browder in 2015, who took his own life after being held for 33 months at Rikers Island on specious charges, lent impetus to a sustained grassroots movement to close the penal colony and replace it with no new carceral facilities. That is, until a cash-flush network of nonprofit organizations tied to the philanthropic juggernaut Ford Foundation got involved, arguing that in addition to closing Rikers, the city needed to open a network of neighborhood-based jails, designed by social justice architects in collaboration with formerly incarcerated people. These organizations, led by JustLeadership USA, turned the goal of closing Rikers Island into a campaign for a network of skyscraper jails throughout New York City.[21]

From an abolitionist perspective these reforms did not meet the non-reformist criterion, since they strengthened the legitimacy of the carceral state while expanding its capacity to hold people captive. The abolitionists argued instead that the $9 billion set aside for the new jails could be invested instead in building up infrastructure in the working-class Black and Latinx communities most highly represented in the city jail population. The coalition No New Jails NYC, comprised of a variety of abolitionists, including veterans of CR, drafted an impressive critique of the plan and their own program for how Rikers could be closed, with no new additional jails opened, and the money saved reinvested through a panoply of social programs addressing common root causes of incarceration, including homelessness, drug addiction, and poverty.[22] No New Jails agitated at community meetings and attempted to popularize an alternative vision for how society could work. The bitter year-long debate between the abolitionist group and a host of the pro-jail carceral nonprofits culminated in the city agreeing to build new jails, with no commitment to closing Rikers. It was cold comfort to the abolitionists that they had predicted this very outcome. While the abolitionists did not block the jail plan, it was nonetheless impressive that a small group of dedicated activists were able to shift the political terrain so markedly that politicians and media figures had to answer to abolitionist arguments in the popular discourse. This kind of practical orientation put abolitionists in position to intervene effectively when the George Floyd Rebellion broke out.

Abolitionism in the George Floyd Rebellion

The abolitionist conquest of the George Floyd Rebellion's political imagination was by no means predestined. The burning of the Third Precinct may have quite literally abolished a piece of carceral infrastructure, but it did not follow at all the political rituals and lexicon of contemporary abolitionism. This has led commentator Adrian Wohlleben to distinguish between prison abolitionism and "prison demolitionism," the practice of directly laying siege to carceral infrastructure and destroying it. Wohlleben, who argues against the mediation of struggle through civil society institutions, writes:

> By contrast with the abolitionist campaigns to "defund" police departments or (in its weaker versions) to supplement them with "civilian review boards"—discursive, dialogical, and demand-based frameworks that leave the initiative in the hands of the state—*demolitionism* aims to materially flatten the organs of state power, to make it logistically and socially impossible for the police and courts to assert their claim to rule; in short, to render the situation ungovernable, and to make this fact *flagrant* for all to see.[23]

Wohlleben argues that the early days of the rebellion represented the opportunity to generalize this attack on the carceral state by repeating the action of the precinct siege, thus spreading the tactic like a meme. This account is particularly compelling as it helps explain how practices like frontliner tactics, and much of its material equipage, spread across the world, in the absence of any particular political theory or organization holding it all together.

In the rebellion's earliest days, another contender, a politically liberal BLM offshoot called Campaign Zero, launched the #8CantWait program, which proposed a list of procedural reforms promising "to bring immediate change to police departments." They include: a ban on chokeholds and strangleholds, a ban on shooting at moving vehicles, mandatory police "de-escalation" in volatile confrontations, mandatory verbal warnings before cops can shoot, cops exhausting all alternatives before shooting, and mandatory intervention by fellow cops witnessing excessive force. The object of this campaign, which was usually associated with a popular proponent, BLM entrepreneur and DC mayoral candidate DeRay McKesson, was improving the oversight of the existing policing infrastructure by investing it with more capacity to train cops, monitor their behavior, and, effectively, police itself. In response, #8toAbolition released a set of demands to defund the police—significantly diminishing the budget of departments, to thereby lessen the scope and power of policing as a key agent of the carceral state.

The abolitionist critiques of #8CantWait represented a profound understanding of the failure of previous efforts at police reform. While it may seem as though increasing police departments' capacity to oversee individual cops is a positive step toward lessening police violence, rank-and-file U.S. police have proven remarkably resistant to the oversight of their actions, especially by civilian leadership. Nebulous programs such as "community policing" are often funded as a means of improving police behavior—and more importantly, their legitimacy, as community policing blends policing strategy with public relations designed to reverse the well-deserved public contempt of cops. But given how opaque these concepts are, and how unaccountable their application, in practice this amounts to more money for cops to do what they were doing before, while placating activists for a little while, until the next major case of police violence. Many observers noted that key reforms demanded by #8CantWait were already on the books in major cities across the u.s., where they were regularly ignored. Abolitionist critics also noted that these reforms would have the effect of strengthening police capacity by investing more of the social wealth into police departments, ostensibly as a means of making them more accountable. Instead, they simply expand the scope of police power, the size of police budgets, and, ultimately, the reach of the carceral state.

Charting a middle path between demolitionism and liberal reform, abolitionists opted for more traditional protests and pushed demand-based campaigns in place of direct confrontations with the state. Simultaneously, they provided their own conception of reform in the place of that offered by #8CantWait. Inspired by "divest/invest" campaigns that pre-dated the rebellion, abolitionists advocated for local initiatives that would diminish public funding of police departments through liberal democratic political channels, and transfer this money into social spending. Defund initiatives gained traction in Minneapolis, Chicago, Los Angeles, and cities and towns across the u.s. The word "defund" was soon ubiquitous at protests across the country, bespeaking a remarkable propaganda victory for the abolitionists. While the organized campaigns for defunding local police departments were infused with momentum in the summer, their longer-term fate has been uneven, and most have largely proven fruitless.

In the time since the summer of 2020, the Defund movement's most auspicious victory has become its most demoralizing defeat. The Minneapolis City Council pledged, in the early days of the rebellion, to completely dismantle its police department, which was at the time seen as a major policy victory. In the time since, however, it has been quietly walked back and ultimately abandoned. This is a common story. A study from January 2021 conducted by Bloomberg CityLab found that while the fifty largest U.S. cities had reduced expenditure on their police forces in their 2021 budgets, this fell within the across-the-board cuts made amid the economic ravages of COVID, and the portion of general expenditures going to police departments actually rose 0.1 percent. In Seattle, where the city council voted to cut the police budget in half, they could only muster an 11.2 percent cut, and Minneapolis, which had attempted to lead the pack nationally, cut its police budget by 14.8 percent, part of a total city budget cut of 6.7 percent.[24] As of writing, it is clear that campaigns to defund the police by public policy maneuvering have largely come to naught.

Of course, as Wohlleben concedes, the dynamic driving demolitionism played itself out quickly in the rebellion. To this we will add that the horizon for sustained attack on carceral infrastructure never even opened in the vast majority of places where protests occurred; demolitionism was only practiced by small groups of people in a small fraction of the cities where protests were held. This absence of direct confrontation with the carceral state left the field open for the experimentation of longer-term projects, capable of keeping momentum going as the fires of the first few weeks subsided or had never arrived. Both approaches, then, while inspiring in different ways, could not accomplish their goals and died out. Defund campaigns, however "realistic" they might be according to their proponents, also appear to have had a short life. While supporters can argue that Defund campaigns are in it for the long haul, change does not come overnight, and the fact is that they don't have much to show for their efforts. This is very unlikely to change so long as their strategy remains reliant on

the carceral state willfully reforming itself based on the persuasive moral arguments of organizers and episodic adventures in
electioneering.

Starve the Pigs

"Invest funds diverted from police and prisons," write the authors
of the collective statement "Choosing Real Safety,"

> toward building safety for those most impacted by surveil-
> lance and policing: Black, Indigenous, unhoused, migrant,
> people who use [criminalized] drugs, and people living with
> disabilities. This includes investments in long-term free and
> affordable housing for all, access to free and healthy food,
> clean water, and community gardens for all, free public tran-
> sit, harm-reduction supports for drug users, childcare, free
> post-secondary education, and regularization of migrants/
> status for all.[25]

A primary demand of Defund campaigns is to shift funding to
other social institutions that ostensibly build healthy and safe
communities, such as public schools. The demands "Schools
Not Jails" and "Books Not Bars" have long been abolitionist
rallying cries. However, as Camille E.S.A. Acey wrote in CR's
special issue of *Social Justice*, we cannot assume that non-carceral
social institutions, including schools, are politically neutral.
Instead, they are important social institutions for safeguarding
and reproducing the social order that police enforce.[26] Not only
does education seek to imbue civic myths of u.s. exceptionalism
and the righteousness of imperialism in even the most apathetic
student, but it actively inculcates the discipline necessary to
ensure a docile and unquestioning working class stratified
along racial lines—or else mark students from a young age as
malcontents ripe for the school-to-prison pipeline. The same can

be said of public housing, public assistance, social work, and any number of other social institutions under capitalism that may seem appealing after decades of austerity but which have their historical roots in class domination, and have today become an important aspect of how the shadow carceral state operates.

Similarly, activists involved in such campaigns as Counselors Not Cops attempt to counterbalance the harmful presence of police in schools by increasing spending on social workers. However, both inside and outside schools, social workers can be petty tyrants, befitting their historical role as managers of working people on behalf of the ruling class, even when they share a racialized background with those they manage. The same goes for public assistance; exploring the long history of the welfare rights struggle in America demonstrates how inextricably bound up together the welfare and penal state are. This makes for less catchy political slogans, but it is an important reality that we must grapple with as today's Defund campaigns imagine decreasing the scope and size of the penal state to invest it in welfare spending. However, the penal and welfare arms of the state are often indistinguishable in their institutional practices of stigmatizing, criminalizing, and punishing the poor. Access to welfare is a humiliating process that constantly pushes poor people to prove their worth and work low-wage jobs in exchange for minimal cash relief. The welfare system makes one feel like a criminal. Anyone who has been to a Food Stamp facility in a Black neighborhood has likely beheld largely Black social workers heaping derision and abuse on largely Black recipients.

For a working-class person, the threat of incarceration and the disciplinary imperative to complete a mandated program at the local welfare office to meet workfare requirements serve the same punitive function. Even if these services are not so directly connected to the punishment system, they are still part of the same disciplinary regime rooted in a necessity to force working people to adopt degrading, exploitative labor and not challenge the broader social order. The violence and humiliation of forced socialization via public schools follows much of the same imperative. It is a curious fact of contemporary leftism that the above argument is common knowledge—even those who haven't read Foucault's *Discipline and Punish* know it is no coincidence that *"prisons resemble* factories, schools, barracks, hospitals, which all *resemble prisons"*—but many nonetheless offer defenses of welfare, public education, and other disciplinary institutions as somehow antithetical to the brutality of capitalist society.[27] When abolitionist Kay Gabriel refers to public services as "institutions that sustain people and communities," it is hard not to rebut that these institutions sustain people and communities in a very particular way, suitable for the needs of capital.[28] How much can u.s. health care, schooling, and the dehumanizing public assistance system ever be extricated from the brutal class relation they serve to reproduce? Central to the state services that many abolitionists argue should take the place of prisons and police is the figure of class domination.

Of course, there is a difference in kind between agents of capitalist coercion who deal only in violence, and others who work through subtler means, such as the provision of basic amenities. Granting this distinction, however, it is a mistake to assume that empowering the soft side of coercion instead of the hard one will empower people in any meaningful sense. The nineteenth-century pioneers of the nonprofit sector such as Josephine Shaw Lowell developed intricate systems for enforcing the deference and docility of people seeking basic amenities like food and firewood, who were forced to demonstrate they were "worthy" of aid, meaning they adhered to labor market discipline and respected the social hierarchy. These charity pioneers, who laid the foundation for modern social work, were acutely aware of the danger of communist movements to the capitalist order, especially after the Paris Commune, and did everything they could to discourage workers from demanding means of subsistence not as a privilege to be gained through the approval of their social betters, but as a right.

Another common argument among abolitionists—taken up by Bernie Sanders—claims that it is cheaper to send a person to a fancy college for four years than it is to incarcerate them for the same amount of time. This is used as evidence of the irrationality of incarceration. But this formulation isn't nearly as clever as some activists think. The state does not need to incarcerate every single senior at a given high school for prison to serve the basic function of absorbing redundant or recalcitrant proletarians, disciplining others to fit into the lowest tiers of the labor market, warehousing others, and threatening the rest with harsh treatment should they break the law. Abolitionists like Ruth Wilson Gilmore have long argued that mass incarceration is an austerity measure. Amid a decades-long capitalist crisis beginning in the 1970s, police and prisons have proven cheaper for the ruling class than guaranteeing free health care, housing, and education, and other minimum demands for a comfortable life. The ruling class in its present moribund state has proven belligerently unwilling to provide even the bare minimum subsistence for workers in the U.S. and is perhaps merely incapable due to the persistent crisis of profitability that has beleaguered global capital since the 1970s.

Regardless of whether capitalism can ultimately afford to provide a comfortable life for all—a question, in any case, that only makes sense when addressed by concrete class struggle—it is clear that in deploying prisons and police to manage the lives of working people, money is being saved. Further, it is impossible to understand the political benefits that the ruling class enjoys by making the working class feel powerless and entitled to just about nothing. Even the laudable idea of free college for all says nothing about what jobs would be available, given that the current labor market is already oversaturated with college-educated workers at the present levels of education. The juxtaposition of prison costs and college tuition might make for effective propaganda, calling attention to the repressive basis of u.s. social order, but it should not be taken literally. Even reducing police budgets to zero across the country and redistributing the funds to the people most in need of resources would be a drop in the bucket compared to the vast inequality that characterizes our society and will persist as long as we have a society stratified along the lines of class. If abolitionists pick these kinds of issues as a rhetorical device, to illustrate the deprivations of capitalist society through the Socratic method, they may be injecting even more confusion into the matter than clarity, since plots to escape capitalist society in a piecemeal fashion don't make any sense.

Contrary to rhetoric emphasizing the folly of spending on jail beds versus mortarboards, the carceral state is not a big mistake; it is the way that capitalism has kept itself propped up through decades of economic crisis and challenges from below, especially the revolutionary movement of the 1960s. "It's not broken," abolitionist Pilar Maschi recently argued. "It works very well."[29] Abolitionists who channel their activity into petitioning state institutions and jockeying for power on the granular level within government bureaucracies are effectively demanding that a system that is propped up by cops and prisons voluntarily do away with prisons and cops. This is due in large part to the persistent belief, particularly among academics and social media pundits who overestimate their own social importance, that persuasive moral arguments made with righteous fervor will make the state realize the error of the policies by which it has comfortably managed the working class on behalf of capital for decades.

It is a telling bellwether of the moment that Alex Vitale's book *The End of Policing* has attained such a wide readership among people searching for structural analysis of the carceral state. In particular, Vitale aims to outline the historical role of u.s. police in maintaining the color line and reproducing capitalist social relations. *The End of Policing* presents a withering critique of the harm cops cause working-class communities, especially those of color, throughout U.S. society, and should be read by anyone still possessed of the antiquated prejudice that police have any positive social function. Vitale persistently argues that the cops are simply not socially useful. There is, however, a contradiction between Vitale's insistence that the police do not make any sense as social actors, and the clear social role that cops play in service of the ruling class. As Maschi argues, the carceral state is doing exactly what it is meant to do, police and all. This tension becomes problematic as Vitale urges that police be abolished through broad-based campaigns with local political machines and nonprofit organizations which carry out the business of the ruling class and have no incentive to change anything on the structural level.[30] Vitale is clear about who the important social actors are in the struggle for abolition as he sees it: "It's about rallying city council members and mayors," he told NPR in the immediate aftermath of the Third Precinct siege, "around a new vision of creating healthier communities."[31] Ultimately, while Vitale's scholarship is helpful in introducing newcomers to critical appraisals of the carceral state, it is hindered by the same illusions that underscore the police reform initiatives of which he is so rightly critical: namely, that we can rely on the system to fix itself.

A Slow Build?

Orienting revolutionary praxis not only requires a long-term vision but is a matter of the tactics used in the short term, and how they change the nature of the struggle. Any political work, no matter how righteous the issue, that puts lawyers, technocrats, academics—and to this we will add social-media stars—in the most vital positions, is empowering the wrong people. This practice is not often carried out deliberately but follows inevitably from strategies that rely on mounting legal challenges or proposing elaborate policy fixes that are the domain of movement managers and not masses of people. "The best way to think about the law is as a shield, not a sword," write labor militants Staughton Lynd and Daniel Gross.[32] The real weapon is collective power, not technical knowledge of how to navigate the boss's system. And as Steve Jenkins argues in a controversial essay about his experiences working at the nonprofit organization Make the Road, a legal or technocratic strategy ultimately empowers a small group of experts and disempowers just about everyone else. This is so regardless of the rhetoric that many such organizations put forward about being led by the most directly impacted people, or how many people are mobilized to attend rallies organized in the service of a strategy over which they have no meaningful control.[33] These critiques could be readily applied to abolitionist campaigns that emphasize working within municipal budgeting processes or lobbying politicians, using legalistic methods *as a sword and not a shield.*

Entering any partnership with public administration is a fraught undertaking for movements for human liberation. No logical, humane, or empathetic person could administer a society as despicable as that of the United States without losing themselves completely in the cynical morass of realpolitik. Participatory budgetary allocation is no different. "Once we accede to opening the books," write Jocelyn Cohn and James Frey,

> we have entered enemy terrain . . . It can be demonstrated through the magic of spreadsheets that our demands are simply unaffordable. There will be information that cannot be revealed to us, or is beyond our comprehension, which demonstrates this irrefutably. The money just isn't there![34]

By contrast, when movements are powerful enough to make actual demands they should not concern themselves with how these demands are met. It is a perennial miracle of riots and rebellions, seen most recently in Biden's massive spending plans, that money magically appears for a host of social spending that was inconceivable before, when the money supposedly wasn't there. From a revolutionary perspective, capitalist society will never meet the ultimate "demand," which is its own abolition, so working together with the ruling class to administer society can only go so far.

What piecemeal efforts can achieve quite concretely is the legitimation of the very institutions which abolitionism should work to discredit, such as bourgeois democracy. Regardless of what individual abolitionists might believe about the irreconcilability of abolitionism and the capitalist state, the message sent by reliance on city councils and woke politicians is quite clear: these institutions *can* be made to serve working people's needs. This mystification also allows for career politicians to posture as friends of the movement, for as long as it is politically expedient, shedding abolitionism at the first opportunity, as happened with the Defund campaigns. It is understandable why many revolutionary-minded people engage with these institutions; when you become dedicated to the total defeat of the ruling class, the entirety of society becomes the terrain of battle. Abstention from parliamentary or trade union bureaucracies on the grounds of principle alone is just as indefensible as relying on them exclusively. But the action revolutionaries undertake within these organs of capitalist rule should serve to delegitimize these enemy institutions and ultimately supersede them, replacing them with great movements against the capitalist social order they serve to prop up. This is what abolitionists such as DSA Emerge appear to believe they are doing when supporting liberal political candidates, in the name of communism. And this might be true. But it is always worthwhile to ask: who is playing whom?

Further, the awareness of how dependency on funding can defang radical projects is an ongoing concern in abolitionist circles, since it's highly unlikely the ruling class will finance its own overthrow. The presence of nonprofits throughout the abolitionist landscape is, accordingly, not to be taken lightly. If we follow scholar Jennifer Wolch to consider the nonprofit sector a "shadow state," it is worth especially considering how—if at all—working within nonprofits, especially large ones funded and controlled by the ruling class, differs from working within the state to secure the strength and versatility of capitalism amid a period of prolonged social crisis.[35] This is especially true with the rise of the diversity industry and a generation of young nonprofit managers, including those hailing from working-class communities of color, and who speak the language of abolition and even revolution but often represent nothing more than the present iteration of Josephine Shaw Lowell and her cohort of middle-class managers of working-class life. "The more a dominant class is able to absorb the best people from the dominated classes," writes Marx, "the more solid and dangerous is its rule."[36]

In particular, re-reading *The Revolution Will Not Be Funded* today furnishes many insights but also points to some limits of this classic work. More than a few of the essays explain the reformism of the nonprofit sector by citing the racial and gender composition of organizations' managers, and the lack of people in leadership positions who are directly affected by the issues the nonprofits address. To evaluate this theory in 2021, one need only look at an organization such as JustLeadership USA (JLUSA), which was the key motivating force behind the NYC jail expansion discussed above. JLUSA was founded by Glenn Martin, a formerly incarcerated Black man, under the banner "the people closest to the problem are the ones closest to the solution." The organization represents itself as being led by "directly impacted people," and used all the right buzzwords from the abolition playbook. Similarly, activists with No New Jails NYC—the abolitionist challenger to JLUSA—were baited as inauthentic outsiders, while the forces campaigning for a network of new cages portrayed themselves as the real representatives of "the community." The use of the language of abolition to sell New York City on new jails, advocated by "directly impacted" people and community organizations with people of color in leadership positions, is just the latest proof that reducing the correctness of politics to the identity of the speaker is not just tokenizing, it is a political dead end.

Relatedly, the practical nature of u.s. abolitionism risks creating an almost-religious emphasis on *slow, patient work*. Abolitionists commonly insist on a vision of social change that is not a matter of abrupt, revolutionary transformations, but "that journey, that practice, that slow build," which incrementally links practices of reform and community building into a vanishing horizon somewhere far off in the future, or maybe even never.[37] It is not uncommon to meet an abolitionist who admits that they don't imagine their vision ever coming to fruition, and instead see abolition as a perennial process of correcting the ills of capitalist society—which is of course a textbook definition of liberal democracy, espoused proudly by no less a standard bearer of bourgeois democracy than Immanuel Kant. Others argue for simply making people's lives better, which is laudable. But whatever crumbs people get today can be attributed to militant struggle in the streets—such as the conflict in the streets of Ferguson, Missouri, which set the agenda for the present moment more than the decades of peaceful reformist activist that preceded it. The fact that groups more inclined toward policy reforms, including the national Black Lives Matter network, were able to subsequently use the Ferguson rebellion to build more traditional leftist campaigns does not detract from the source of that movement in the rioting and confrontational actions of the people of Ferguson.

While the slow build might be a necessary component of revolutionary organizing, so too is orienting to the moment of a decisive break. Given that many struggles catch like wildfire, changing large numbers of peoples' tactical and strategic horizons virtually overnight—as we saw in the George Floyd Rebellion—there is a lurking danger in the consistent emphasis abolitionists place on a gradualist conception of social change. The George Floyd Rebellion should give pause to those who still adhere to abolitionism's emphasis on a long and protracted road of reform leading to radical reconfiguration of society in the distant future; in the very least, there should be a place in this praxis for moments of monumental social upheaval.

The idea that dramatic social changes are achieved through an amalgamation of piecemeal measures, rather than moments of great social upheaval, is historically suspect. Slavery was not abolished by the numerous reformers who sought to regulate it and make it more humane over time. Abolitionists defined themselves *against* what they perceived to be the gradualism of the wider anti-slavery movement. Abolitionism required the decisive action of runaway slaves, renegade abolitionists such as John Brown, and a great war. As Noel Ignatiev argued, John Brown's attack on the armory at Harper's Ferry "was not an aberration but the logical application of the abolitionist strategy," setting in motion a chain of events that brought the long-simmering conflict to a head.[38] The abolitionist movement spread its message through constant propagandizing: speeches, writing in newspapers, and periodicals, and of course relying on popular visual materials to appeal to the masses, which included cartoons, lithographs, and engravings. William Lloyd Garrison's newspaper *The Liberator* defined what had drawn a critical mass of Black and white men, women, and children to abolitionism. Its adherents were not interested in gradual reform; they wanted the outright end of slavery by any means necessary. They did not seek conciliation with slave owners or compromises with the politicians who represented them; they agitated for outright abolition, which they knew would require the head-on defeat of the power bloc that benefited from it, not changing their minds.

In his classic study of revolutionary theory, *Notes on Dialectics*, C.L.R. James argues that moments of great decision—we think of the burning of the Third Precinct—are not achieved by the gradual politicizing of people through one reform after another. Nor are they the result of masses of people acting based on their education by popular leaders. Instead, these are instances when great contradictions long unfolding beneath the appearance of social peace explode dramatically into the foreground, changing in the process what people think is possible. The widespread anti-police sentiment that the rebellion demonstrated did not arise the day the precinct was burned. It has long simmered beneath the surface of an official culture obsessed with police worship, and a panoply of liberal institutions, including much of the original incarnation of Black Lives Matter, fixated on the Sisyphean task of "police reform." Beneath these stale politics, a new reality simmered. James distills this point with a piece of marginalia from Lenin's notes on Hegel: "LEAP LEAP LEAP LEAP."[39] The new reality beneath the old forms announces itself, changing the terrain of the possible in the process. "No one in the world dreamt that underneath the France of 1789 had developed the passion for equality which was to burst forth in the French Revolution," James writes in *American Civilization*, "and help tear down the age-old structure of monarchy, aristocracy, and clergy."[40]

Tellingly, it often occurs that when objective conditions, like the low-scale social war which characterizes the onslaught of the carceral state, facilitate a great "LEAP" such as the siege of the Third Precinct, the most active participants have nothing to do with any of the activism that has preceded it, and might even be hostile to it. This last part is especially true when self-identified activist veterans, with all their rituals, social baggage, and fidelity to a certain type of politics quickly being eclipsed, attempt to parachute in and pull rank on the newcomers, telling them that they're doing it wrong. The George Floyd Rebellion had no shortage of gatekeepers who descended on large and unruly marches with megaphones, intent on disciplining the rebellious masses into their own anachronistic understanding of how struggle should play out. This practice even earned a name: swooping. Instead of gatekeeping, what the present movement needs from experienced activists and militants is assistance in working out its own questions, novel to a new moment, and finding adequate forms of political organization and struggle that do not come down from the past but meet the needs of the present. By virtue of capturing the imagination of the George Floyd Rebellion, abolitionism in particular finds itself at a crossroads.

The Crossroads of Revolution and Reform

"Before abolitionism, there was revolutionary struggle," writes veteran abolitionist Joy James in the essay "Airbrushing Revolution for the Sake of Abolition," published in the thick of the George Floyd Rebellion. James does not argue that the two figures are inherently antithetical. However, she describes how a movement born out of the working-class struggle led by Black and Latinx revolutionaries in the 1960s gave way to a largely academic milieu, rooted in celebrity, respectability, and alliances with the ruling class. To underscore this point, she cites Angela Davis's inclusion of Obama within the "Black Radical Tradition" alongside Assata Shakur, despite the fact that the former's Department of Justice subsequently treated the latter as a wanted terrorist on par with Al-Qaeda, while largely pursuing the neoliberal policies of his predecessors that made life increasingly worse for working-class Black people. "Elites offer more peer-recognition to progressive (or conservative) associates than to working-class militants," James writes. "The political economy of social justice produces employment, honoraria, royalties, and stellar salaries, generating personal wealth or portfolio management with low risk of surveillance and repression."[41] Just as James outlines how the fuzzy political boundaries of academic radicalism produced widespread support for capitalist politicians like Obama, we can see how the contemporary movement of abolitionism can be twisted to become antithetical to social revolution.

The revolutionary abolitionist tradition Joy James evokes instructs us that capitalism, not bad ideas or mistaken priorities, lies at the root of the racist violence endemic to u.s. society. The Emerge caucus of the Democratic Socialists of America argues this explicitly: "We are fighting for a world without police and prisons," they write.

> But abolition isn't just about the absence of police and prisons, it also means the presence of well-resourced communities, with housing and food and care workers, and of community practices that prevent and keep us accountable for harm. So abolition is about divesting from police and prisons, and it's also about investing in communities, particularly Black and Brown communities impacted by the systemic violence of policing and prisons. These resources, which all communities deserve, are the greatest violence prevention of all. We are fighting for a communist and abolitionist future—a society built not on the violence of a state designed to protect property and capital, but one in which people are in power to provide for each other.[42]

However, Emerge, which focuses the lion's share of its attention on electoral campaigns at the local level, does not elaborate on how it understands communism, or how campaigns, such as those to defund the police, serve as a bridge to get there. Whether they imagine communism will be achieved by a violent social revolution or accomplished through the legislative channels in which they presently work is largely set aside. Above all, it is not clear how any of the social transformations Emerge champions can be the result of demand campaigns mediated through liberal democratic institutions, instead of seized directly by working people who have effected a dramatic break with capitalist parliamentarianism. Here we encounter a question of the chicken and egg.

Emerge member Kay Gabriel writes, in a sophisticated defense of Defund,

> If we are going to achieve a world in which people are not forced *en masse* to wither in cages, where police and racist vigilantes do not murder with impunity, where racial capitalism no longer consigns some people to slow or rapid deaths for the benefit of another class's ever-expanding wealth, then we will have to begin, but not end, with the mass transfer of resources away from state violence and towards institutions that sustain people and communities.

Gabriel argues stridently against liberals who claim that the campaign to defund the police does not have a pragmatic approach to politics. She argues instead that Defund campaigns point toward a post-capitalist society. "*We do not have to live this way,*" Gabriel suggests, "and Defund plots a course to collectively do otherwise." Gabriel's examples bolstering this claim are grassroots political campaigns that have righteous aims— removing cops from schools, subways, and public housing—but have not won anything. These groups make righteous demands, but nobody with any power is listening. And why would they? Unions, nonprofits, and political parties in this country are structurally arrayed against granting anything but the most perfunctory crumbs to working people. They are institutions thoroughly enmeshed in capitalism that function above all to ensure its safety. How will this change? By contrast, Gabriel argues that organizing should be aimed at creating "structures of community self-determination that make policing obsolete."[43] We concur. But what are these structures? Will they exist within a society governed by the wage relation and production for exchange, in other words, within capitalism? And if not, how will the capitalist mode of production, and the nation states that uphold it, be brought to an end?

Similarly, legal scholar Amna A. Akbar has argued the demand to defund the police is part of a broader program of "revolutionary" social transformation. "The demand for defunding," Akbar writes, "shifts power and our imaginations away from the police and toward a society rooted in collective care for ordinary people. It brings into sharp relief who we have allowed ourselves to become and offers a vision for who we could be."[44] What does this mean in concrete terms for people energized by the George Floyd Rebellion and seeking to effect revolutionary change in the world? The same problem arises at the conclusion of a splendid essay on the George Floyd Rebellion by critic Tobi Haslett. After mounting a spirited defense of rioting and looting for a presumably liberal audience, and claiming the distinct revolutionary potential of the rebellion, Haslett argues that the rebels of 2020 must fuse with the Bernie Sanders movement. "It's impossible to say what comes next, either for the Black movement against state terror or the state-facing redistributive effort," Haslett writes,

> but short of a defeat of capital in a single, stunning stroke, any left that hopes to assemble its flailing forces must find a way to join the two clearest fronts of conflict: on one hand build class power by wresting benefits from the state, on the other slay the beast that eats the dark and poor.[45]

If this means simply working through liberal democratic channels to mitigate the effects of poverty and structural racism, the case for this approach needs to be made as distinct from the ordinary neoliberal technocracy Democrats are already engaged in. If the solution is social revolution, it is imperative to outline how actions in the here and now connect to that horizon.

"Abolition," write Emerge, "calls on us to build collective political power both apart from and against oppressive structures."[46] This formulation clearly evokes the theory of "dual power," as first theorized by V. I. Lenin in 1917. Regardless of what one thinks of Lenin, dual power represents a coherent revolutionary strategy for suppressing by force the institutions of bourgeois society by creating popular alternative institutions. It is of course coincidence to unearth coherent revolutionary strategy in contemporary abolitionist praxis, given its origins in the revolutionary movements of the 1960s. However, it is at present in need of development and extrapolation, especially around the question of the state. Is the state the means through which we effect revolutionary change, a tool to be seized and repurposed? Or is the state inherently an adversary to the realization of a post-capitalist society? These questions are not idle, as they pertain to how we relate to the state in the present, and whether such efforts as running candidates for office or fighting to control city budgets promotes, or hinders, the creation of the society abolitionists envision.

A stark line of demarcation is drawn by Shemon Salam in an essay from July 2020. "There are two kinds of abolition," he writes: "revolutionary abolition and reformist abolition." Revolutionary abolition is defined as "the self-activity of the proletariat in fighting against the entire carceral logic of the state and racial capitalism. This includes burning down police stations, destroying cop cars, attacking police officers, and redistributing goods from Target and Versace." To this, he counterposes "a reformist abolition," which sees "politicians as the principal historical actors, in relation to whom it positions itself as a pressure group. In this way, reformist abolitionism removes proletarians from the terrain of struggle."[47] We share the spirit of Salam's intervention, just as we shared the frustration of outright rebellion giving way to large crowds sitting down helplessly before lines of riot cops, forced to listen to bad poetry while the embers of the Third Precinct still smoldered. Salam's distinction is surely keeping with Joy James in upholding the revolutionary heritage of abolitionism as adhering in direct insurrectionary confrontation with the carceral state.

Could it really be, however, that the only activity with any revolutionary potential is the direct physical confrontation with the carceral state? A small core of militants unafraid of violence may be an essential component of a revolution but will not be the sum, and this is doubly so of young people being politicized through this moment, who just months prior had pinned all their hopes on Bernie Sanders, or nothing at all. Further, Salam's proposition presents us with the demoralizing prospect that only a tiny fraction of the street activity in 2020 had any proto-revolutionary content, and that a minuscule portion of Americans were acting in any way that can be seen to prefigure participation in a large-scale revolution. What was everyone else doing? Did the massive, unprecedented marches in solidarity with the burning of the Third Precinct and the general opposition to the carceral state serve only a recuperative function? Or was there something more complicated going on, a movement between these two poles? Is there anything potentially revolutionary in what Salam dubs the reformist abolition camp?

A helpful litmus test for divining revolutionary abolitionism from reformism comes from the movement's own conceptual toolbox. Drawing on Du Bois, Angela Davis has articulated abolitionism as a continuation of Reconstruction, and in particular, the tradition of "abolitionist democracy" begun in the aftermath of the Civil War.[48] But the meaning of Reconstruction is not assured, even among those who claim to take up its mantle. This point was made compellingly in a 1991 essay by Noel Ignatiev, himself a lifelong devotee of Du Bois. Ignatiev challenged the pervasive reading of Reconstruction offered by historian Eric Foner, according to which it was an unfinished bourgeois revolution. Citing Du Bois' insistence on the slaves as "workers," their abandonment of plantations as a "general strike," and Reconstruction as tending toward "the dictatorship of the proletarian," Ignatiev argues that while we must indeed pursue the unfinished business of Reconstruction, it will not mean the attainment of formal equality under liberal democracy, as Foner argues, but the abolition of class society itself.[49] We believe that this distinction presents a simple crossroads facing contemporary abolitionism, alongside a handy metric for evaluating the politics of abolitionists and their projects alike.

Some of this work is already being done. As Salam argues, distinct practices of revolutionary abolitionism characterized the most militant confrontations in the summer of 2020. Additionally, the Revolutionary Abolitionist Movement (RAM), an organization fusing themes of U.S. abolitionism with insurrectionary anarchism, has established small chapters in cities across the United States.[50] Organizations like the Haters represent an insurrectionary tradition within Black struggle stretching back to at least Robert F. Williams and the Revolutionary Action Movement of the 1960s, and continuing through the Panthers and the Black Liberation Army.[51] Simultaneously, the SM28 (Spirit of May 28th) Collective is attempting to craft an explicitly revolutionary approach grounded in the novelty of the George Floyd Rebellion.[52] In short, the revolutionary tradition that helped create abolitionism is not extinct. These efforts, however, remain exceptions to a mainstream current of abolitionism that is far more opaque on the question of reform versus revolution, when not outright supportive of reform in practice. The contradiction within abolitionism must be resolved. At present, the praxis of mainstream abolitionism could not have produced the George Floyd Rebellion. We can speculate that many would have even tried to stop the burning of the Third Precinct had they had sufficient numbers on the scene, in the name of a slow build and keeping people safe. Deepening struggle in the future will require a qualitative shift in how abolition is understood by the majority of its adherents. This work is already underway, but must be amplified and redoubled in the months and years ahead.

Abolitionism after George Floyd

"Let it be said clearly," writes Shemon Salam, "the George Floyd Rebellion is the new criterion to which all theories and politics must be held to account."[53] We share this assessment and believe that no politics can avoid assessing its presuppositions in light of the decisive action taken by so many people in the summer of 2020. This is why we have attempted to sketch out the history, strengths, and potential pitfalls of the abolitionist tradition.

In its attack on existing society, abolitionism presents a powerful critique that helps us delegitimize and begin to dismantle the carceral state. It also furnishes an analysis which enables us to treat the history of the carceral state as the history of racialized class domination. Contemporary abolitionism builds on the success of mainstream critiques of the carceral state such as *The New Jim Crow* to present the current state of things as not a response to "crime" but the product of concrete political struggle in which we are engaged whether we like it or not. In this way, the ground is prepared to consider the struggle against the carceral state one component of a necessary social revolution. On the contrary, in its pursuit of reform, even under the banner of "non-reformist reforms," abolitionist organizing risks legitimizing organs of liberal democracy and steering the exciting new energy it has elicited down the same dead-end road of reform that the tradition itself critiques deftly. It is more than a little unnerving to meet abolitionists who express surprise that city councils have heard their message about the righteousness of opposing a jail or defunding the police, and ended up still siding with the carceral state. To feign disbelief for an audience of potentially sympathetic liberals is perhaps a defensible act of political theatrics. But the genuine surprise that bourgeois politicians do not willingly cooperate with the dismantling of the carceral infrastructure that props up capitalism in the United States reveals that, while there's no shortage of abolitionists who want to instruct others in what to read and how to think, the educator too must be educated.

Regardless of where you stand, it's undeniable that abolitionism has captured the spoils of the George Floyd Rebellion. Moving forward, its partisans must clarify the relationship between abolitionist tactics in the present, and the future society abolitionism hopes to bring into existence. The task ahead of them is steering the current momentum abolitionism enjoys into channels that, rather than simply serving as correctives for liberal democracy to fix its problems with the help of avowed anti-capitalists, actually constitute viable counter-power. This is especially important given the present reshuffling, discussed in the last chapter, through which the carceral state is recalibrating itself in ways that might appear to be in keeping with "non-reformist reforms," such as downsizing the u.s. prison population, but are ultimately geared toward strengthening capitalist society in the long run. Helping release people from prison and reducing the amount of police or cages in a society are laudable aims. But these are not revolutionary in themselves, unless they are a part of a broader social movement to replace capitalist society with a new social order based on satisfying the human needs of all, and meeting with great force everything and everyone who stands in the way of this vision. It does the movement for human liberation no favors to collapse these two unproblematically, or to abstract away from the degree of social transformation—and violent struggle—that will be necessary to realize a world without cops and cages. This is a distinction which must be made as a dividing line in the here and now, since its implications do not refer to a distant future, but how we relate to the promises and pitfalls of the present moment.

Abolitionism demonstrated tremendous resonance in the George Floyd Rebellion, providing the political basis on which participants could understand themselves, what they were doing, and what they were fighting for. But with this success comes the responsibility for abolitionists to clarify their politics and develop an explicitly revolutionary praxis befitting the leadership role the rebellion afforded them. As a new generation of rebels looks to abolitionism to make sense of their activity, what they are fighting against, and, most importantly, what they are fighting for, they are owed a clear conception of how the politics of abolitionism relate, in concrete terms, to bringing a new society into being. As Marx reminds us: "The weapon of criticism cannot, of course, replace criticism of the weapon, material force must be overthrown by material force; but theory also becomes a material force as soon as it has gripped the masses."[54]

Afterword

"It's unprecedented," exclaimed Baltimore's State Attorney General Marilyn Mosby, in reaction to a line-up of law enforcement officers, including top brass such as Minneapolis Police Chief Medaria Arradondo, denouncing fellow police officer Derek Chauvin. In 2020, fourteen officers of the same department, many of whom were ranked sergeant or higher, signed an open letter against Chauvin stating that he "failed as a human and stripped George Floyd of his dignity and life."[1] During Chauvin's trial, Chief Arradondo testified: "It's not part of our training, and it's certainly not part of our ethics or values."[2] Police officers and brass turning on their own is indeed unprecedented, given how just a few years prior Minnesota police officers testified in defense of their coworker Jeronimo Yanez, who fatally shot and killed Philando Castile in front of his girlfriend and four-year-old daughter during a traffic stop.

Chauvin's conviction brought to a close, at least for the time being, the most important and militant rebellion of the last four decades. The conviction, however, does not, as many liberals claim, demonstrate a crack in the "blue wall of silence." It is highly unlikely that American courts will begin to systematically prosecute and convict all killer cops. It took a massive rebellion, widespread looting and rioting, and protests involving millions of Americans for the system to convict just one bad cop. Chauvin's conviction should not signal the weakness of the carceral state, but its versatility. As the u.s. revolutionary Don Hamerquist reminded us: "If the verdict hadn't been guilty on all counts, it would have brought into question whether or not the country has a functional ruling class."

Four years of chaos under Trump left activists largely responding to his latest outrage. There were too many fires to put out at any one time. Trump's racist and incendiary law-and-order rhetoric made the Democrats seem like the champions of working-class people by comparison. The threat of purportedly imminent fascism led many radicals to jump ship and establish popular fronts with liberals, the sole purpose of which ended up being to vote Trump out of office. As America's cultural amnesia and the crisis-laden landscape of contemporary capitalism have combined gradually to bury the George Floyd Rebellion beneath the latest chorus of noise, it now seems so long ago that millions of people gathered to demonstrate against the carceral state and put their body on the line to affirm their commitment to a world free of oppression. Abolition, a radical and previously marginal demand, took center stage not through rhetoric alone, but direct action. For a brief moment, many things seemed possible.

But with Trump gone, and the most diverse presidential cabinet in history at the helm of political power, our real enemy has once again made itself evident: the entire ruling class, progressive wing and all. When it comes to placating mass movements toward the stability of capitalist rule, the Democrats are a lot smarter than their opponents. They have already anticipated the demand for federal investment into Black and Latinx communities led by popular front groups such as the Movement for Black Lives (m4bl) and thrown their full weight behind the George Floyd Justice in Policing Act, touted as legislation that will keep better track of police use of force by creating a national registry on police misconduct and reforming qualified immunity for police officers. Of course, the usual legislative meat grinder will almost certainly ensure that it will be another toothless reform effort. Simultaneously, the hope of realizing social democracy for Black and Latinx people by increasing the numbers on the Squad ignores the powerful ruling-class block that will fight to the death to uphold capitalism and the widespread human disposability it necessarily entails.

In the immediate aftermath of the rebellion, abolitionists have thrown their energy into local campaigns to defund the police at a community level and popularizing practices such as transformative justice that address social problems on the interpersonal level. The imperative to eliminate interpersonal harm, and to keep people safe on the individual level, has increasingly come to stand in for building a new society through class struggle that will by no means be safe or devoid of harm. We share the desire to minimize interpersonal harm, but the idea that we can "keep us safe" under capitalism is a dangerous fantasy, as is the notion that we can create a post-capitalist world without confronting head-on the tremendous violence that keeps the present order propped up. Instead, what is necessary is a politics that builds on the strengths of abolitionism—its critique of the carceral state, its practical tools, its orientation to the here and now—coupled with the militant tactics and social innovations of the George Floyd Rebellion and, above all, the correct assessment by its rebels that there is no more talking to be done with emissaries of the carceral state.

The struggle ahead will not be peaceful, safe, or happy. But it will be necessary to get to the other side. And it can be done. The George Floyd Rebellion will light the way. "Have you ever stopped and realized," writes the author of "The Only Way Out Is Always Through the Police," "that you've just spent more time trying to read a boring long-form essay than it took a group of teenagers to destroy an entire business district and bring the largest city in the country to its knees?"[3]

References

Introduction: A Moment of Promise and Pitfalls

1 Karl Marx and Friedrich Engels, *Manifesto of the Communist Party* (New York, 1955), p. 13.
2 Antonio Gramsci, *Selections from the Prison Notebooks of Antonio Gramsci* (London, 1971), p. 276.
3 Idris Robinson, "How It Might Should Be Done," August 16, 2020, https://illwill.com.
4 Jarrod Shanahan and Zhandarka Kurti, "Prelude to a Hot American Summer" (July–August 2020), www.brooklynrail.org.
5 Zhandarka Kurti and Jarrod Shanahan, "Rebranding Mass Incarceration: The Lippman Commission and Carceral Devolution in New York City," *Social Justice*, xlv/2–3 (2018), pp. 25–49.
6 Michel Foucault, *Discipline and Punish: The Birth of the Prison* (New York, 1977).
7 Zhandarka Kurti and Jarrod Shanahan, "Carceral Non-Profits and the Limits of Prison Reform," acme: *Journal for Critical Geographies*, xx/5 (2022), pp. 597–617.

One: A Hot American Summer

1 James Baldwin, *The Fire Next Time* (New York, 1993), p. 76.
2 Inhabit, "Dignity: On the George Floyd Rebellion," June 29, 2020, https://territories.substack.com.
3 Keeanga-Yamahtta Taylor, "The Black Plague," April 16, 2020, www.newyorker.com.
4 John Garvey "Underlying Conditions," April 21, 2020, www.hardcrackers.com.
5 The National Urban League, *The State of Black America Unmasked* (2020), https://soba.iamempowered.com.
6 John Byrne, "Chicago Mayor Lori Lightfoot Spent $281.5 Million in

Federal COVID-19 Relief Money on Police Payroll," *Chicago Tribune*, February 18, 2021.

7 Speech delivered with Malcolm X at the Williams Institutional CME Church, Harlem, New York, December 20, 1964.

8 G. L. Schwartz and J. L. Jahn, "Mapping Fatal Police Violence across U.S. Metropolitan Areas: Overall Rates and Racial/Ethnic Inequities, 2013–2017," *PLOS ONE*, XV/6 (2020).

9 Ibid.

10 Jeff Hargarten et al., "Every Police-Involved Death in Minnesota Since 2000," April 13, 2021, www.startribune.com.

11 Kim Moody, "The Roots of Racist Policing: A View from the United States," July 27, 2020, https://spectrejournal.com.

12 People's Policy Project, "Class and Racial Inequalities in Police Killings," June 23, 2020, www.peoplespolicyproject.org.

13 Jessica Nickrand, "Minneapolis's White Lie," February 21, 2015, www.theatlantic.com; Samuel Stebbins and Michael B. Sauter, "25 Richest Cities in America: Does Your Metro Area Make the List?," May 17, 2018, www.usatoday.com.

14 Samuel L. Myers Jr., "The Minessota Paradox," University of Sam Minnesota, Hubert L. Humphreys School of Public Affairs (2018), www.hhh.umn.edu.

15 Adam McCann, "States with the Biggest and Smallest Wealth Gaps by Race/Ethnicity," January 25, 2022, www.wallethub.com.

16 Greg Rosalasky, "Minneapolis Ranks Near the Bottom for Racial Inequality," June 2, 2020, www.npr.org.

17 Minneapolis Employment and Economic Development, "Twin Cities Metro Regional Disparities by Race and Origin" (2016), www.mngov.org.

18 Rosalsky, "Minneapolis Ranks Near the Bottom for Racial Equality."

19 ACLU, "Picking up the Pieces: Policing in America, A Minneapolis Case Study" (2015), www.aclu.org.

20 MPD 150, "Enough Is Enough: A 150-Year Performance Review of the Minneapolis Police Department" (2017), p. 7, at www.mpd150.com.

21 Samantha Michaels, "Minneapolis Police Union President Allegedly Wore a 'White Power Patch' and Made Racist Remarks," May 30, 2020, www.motherjones.com.

22 Report of the Metro Gang Strike Force Review Panel (2009), Minnesota Department of Public Safety, https://dps.mn.gov.

23 Randy Furst, "Minneapolis' Janeé Harteau Breaking the Mold as Chief of Police," November 28, 2012, www.startribune.com.

24 MPD 150, "Enough Is Enough."

25 Jamiles Lartey and Simone Weichselbaum, "Before George Floyd's Death, Minneapolis Police Failed to Adopt Reforms, Remove Bad Officers," May 28, 2020, www.themarshallproject.org.

26 Minneapolis Police Department 2018, "Focusing on Procedural Justice: Internally and Externally," June 2018, www.insidempd.com.

27 Jeff Hargarten et al., "Every Police Involved Death in Minnesota," January 3, 2022, www.startribune.com.

28 Keeanga-Yamahtta Taylor, *From #BlackLivesMatter to Black Liberation* (Chicago, IL, 2016), p. 80.

29 Larry Buchanan, Quoctrung Bui and Jugal K. Patel, "Black Lives Matter May Be the Largest Movement in U.S. History," July 3, 2020, www.nytimes.com.

30 Abha Bhattarai and Hannah Denham, "Stealing to Survive: More Americans are Shoplifting Food as Aid Runs Out During the Pandemic," December 10, 2014, www.washingtonpost.com.

31 Marie Gottschalk, "Dismantling the Carceral State: The Future of Penal Policy Reform," *Texas Law Review*, LXXXIV/7 (June 2006), pp. 1693–749; Jonathan Simon, "The Rise of the Carceral State," *Social Research*, LXXIV/2 (Summer 2007), pp. 471–508.

32 Anonymous, "The Only Way Out Is Always Through the Police: A History of the Rise and Fall of the 2020 New York Riots," July 15, 2021, www.itsgoingdown.org.

33 See especially Ruth Wilson Gilmore, *Golden Gulag: Prisons, Surplus, Crisis, and Opposition in Globalizing California* (Berkeley, CA, 2007); Tony Platt, *Beyond These Walls: Rethinking Crime and Punishment in the United States* (New York, 2018); Christian Parenti, *Lockdown America: Police and Prisons in the Age of Crisis* (New York, 2000).

34 Loren Goldner, "1973 Redux? Continuity and Discontinuity in the Decline of Dollar-Centered World Accumulation" (2006), www.breaktheirhaughtypower.org.

35 C.L.R. James, *The Black Jacobins: Toussaint L'Ouverture and the San Domingo Revolution* (New York, 1963), p. 138.

36 Unicorn Riot livestream, May 28, 2020, https://unicornriot.ninja.

37 Anonymous, "Dispatch from the Rebellion in Minneapolis," June 1, 2020, https://illwill.com.

38 Tobi Haslett, "Magic Actions: Looking Back on the George Floyd Rebellion," May 7, 2021, www.nplusonemag.com.

39 Armed Conflict Location and Event Data Project (ACLED), "A Year of Racial Justice Protests: Key Trends in Demonstrations Supporting the BLM Movement," May 25, 2021, www.acleddata.com.

40 We discussed this question at length in an interview in September 2020: Jarrod Shanahan and Zhandarka Kurti, "The Shifting Ground: A Conversation on the George Floyd Rebellion," September 20, 2020, https://illwill.com.

41 ACLED, "Demonstrations and Political Violence in America," September 3, 2020, www.acleddata.com.

42 ACLED, "The Future of Stop the Steal: Post-Election Trajectories

for Right-Wing Mobilization in the U.S.," December 10, 2020, www.acleddata.com.

43 Shemon Salam and Arturo Castillon, "Cars, Riots and Black Liberation," November 17, 2020, www.metamute.org.

44 Situationist International, "The Decline and Fall of the Spectacle-Commodity Economy," in *The Situationist International Anthology* (Berkeley, CA, 2006), p. 197. This argument has been taken up by Vicky Osterweil, *In Defense of Looting: A Riotous History of Uncivil Action* (New York, 2020).

45 Slavoj Žižek, "Shoplifters of the World Unite," August 25, 2011, www.lrb.co.uk.

46 For example, historians Eric Hobsbawm, E. P. Thompson, and Peter Linebaugh offer a sophisticated treatment of looting in the context of early capitalist modernity. See Eric Hobsbawm, *Primitive Rebels: Studies in Archaic Forms of Social Movement in the Nineteenth and Twentieth Centuries* (New York, 1965); Peter Linebaugh, *The London Hanged: Crime and Civil Society in the Eighteenth Century* (New York, 2006); Douglas Hay et al., *Albion's Fatal Tree: Crime and Society in Eighteenth Century England* (London, 2011); E. P. Thompson, *Whigs and Hunters: The Origins of the Black Act* (London, 1977).

47 Adrian Wohlleben, "Memes Without End," May 16, 2021, https://illwill.com.

48 Anonymous, "The Siege of the Third Precinct in Minneapolis," June 10, 2020, https://es.crimethinc.com.

49 Chuang, "Welcome to the Frontlines: Beyond Violence and Non-Violence," June 8, 2020, https://chuangcn.org.

50 Anonymous, "The Siege of the Third Precinct."

51 ACLED, "Demonstrations and Political Violence in America."

52 New York Post-Left, "Welcome to the Party: The George Floyd Uprising in NYC," June 24, 2020, www.itsgoingdown.org.

53 Personal conversations between the authors and protestors.

54 Misanthrophile, "Portland Awakens: A Report from the Front Lines," July 21, 2020, https://itsgoingdown.org.

55 Anonymous, "Tools and Tactics in the Portland Protests," August 3, 2020, https://es.crimethinc.com.

56 Misanthrophile, "Portland Awakens."

57 Ibid.

58 Gretchen Kell, "After Floyd's Killing, KIPs at Protests Led to 100-Plus Head Injuries," September 16, 2020, www.news.berkeley.edu.

59 Tim Dickinson, "Trump Claims—and Celebrates—Extrajudicial Killing of Antifa Activist," October 15, 2020, www.rollingstone.com.

60 "First 90 Days of Prisoner Resistance to COVID-19: Report on Events, Data, and Trends," November 12, 2020, www.perilouschronicle.com.

61 Anonymous, "At the Wendy's: Armed Struggle at the End of

the World," November 9, 2020, https://illwill.com; "Onward Barbarians," December 2020, www.endnotes.org.uk.

62 Kuwasi Balagoon, "Brinks Trial: Closing Statement," in *A Soldier's Story: Writings by a Revolutionary New Afrikan Anarchist* (Montreal, 2003).

63 Unicorn Riot livestream.

64 ACLED, "Demonstrations & Political Violence in America."

65 Shemon Salam, "Fanon, Floyd, and Me," May 3, 2021, www.hardcrackers.com.

66 Anonymous, "The World Is Ours: The Minneapolis Uprising in Five Acts," June 12, 2020, www.itsgoingdown.org.

67 Anonymous, "Frontliners to the Front: Between Politics and Rebellion in Atlanta," October 17, 2020, www.itsgoingdown.org.

68 We Still Outside Collective, "On the Black Leadership and Other White Myths," June 4, 2020, https://illwill.com.

69 E. D. Mondainé, "Portland's Protests Were Supposed to Be About Black Lives, Now They're White Spectacle," July 23, 2020, www.washingtonpost.com.

70 Shemon Salam and Arturo Castillon, "The Return of John Brown: White Race Traitors in the 2020 Uprising," September 4, 2020, https://illwill.com.

71 Anonymous, "'Breeway or the Freeway': The Rise of America's Frontliners and Why Louisville Didn't Burn," October 15, 2020, www.itsgoingdown.org.

72 Ben Tobin, "Read What Daniel Cameron Said about the Grand Jury's Findings in the Breonna Taylor Case," September 23, 2020, www.courier-journal.com.

73 Zhandarka Kurti and Jarrod Shanahan, "Justice Department Investigations Don't Actually Challenge Police Violence," April 26, 2021, www.truthout.org.

74 Katie Kim and Lisa Capitanini, "Extremist Groups May be Infiltrating Protests," June 5, 2020, www.nbcchicago.com.

75 Haslett, "Magic Actions."

76 Anonymous, "Frontliners to the Front."

77 Matthew N. Lyons, "Cooptation as a Ruling Class Strategy," June 23, 2020, www.threewayfight.blogspot.com.

78 See in particular Cedric Johnson's *Revolutionaries to Race Leaders: Black Power and the Making of African American Politics* (Minneapolis, MN, 2007); Keeanga-Yamahtta Taylor, *From #BlackLivesMatter to Black Liberation*, pp. 75–106.

79 All Gas No Brakes, "Minneapolis Protest," June 8, 2020, www.youtube.com.

80 Mike O'Meara press conference, June 9, 2020, www.youtube.com.

81 Unicorn Riot livestream.

82 New York Post-Left, "Welcome to the Party."

83 All Gas No Brakes, "Minneapolis Protest."

84 Matthew Impelli, "54 Percent of Americans Think Burning Down Minneapolis Police Precinct Was Justified After George Floyd's Death," June 3, 2020, www.newsweek.com.

85 Haslett, "Magic Actions."

86 Jessica Lussenhop, "George Floyd Death: Why Has a u.s. City Gone Up in Flames?," May 29, 2020, www.bbcnews.co.uk.

87 Chris McGreal, "Anger as Local Police Union Chief Calls George Floyd a 'Violent Criminal,'" June 1, 2020, www.theguardian.com.

88 Martin Kaste, "How Endorsement of Trump Could Affect Legitimacy of Police," October 20, 2020, www.npr.org.

89 Thomas Sugrue, "2020 Is Not 1968: To Understand Today's Protests, You Must Look Further Back," June 11, 2020, www.nationalgeographic.com.

90 See Loren Goldner, *The Remaking of the American Working Class* (1980), at http://breaktheirhaughtypower.org; David Ranney, *New World Disorder: The Decline of u.s. Power* (North Charleston, SC, 2014).

91 Ruth Wilson Gilmore, *Racial Capitalism and the Case for Abolition*, ed. Naomi Murakawa (Chicago, IL, 2021).

92 Cited in TZ, "Burn Down the Prison," December 11, 2014, www.unityandstruggle.org.

93 Zachary Siegel, "'Starve the Beast': A Q&A with Alex S. Vitale on Defunding the Police," June 4, 2020, www.thenation.com.

94 Haslett, "Magic Actions."

95 Phil A. Neel, "The Spira: Epilogue to the French Edition of *Hinterland: America's New Landscape of Class and Conflict*," September 2020, www.brooklynrail.org.

96 Shemon Salam and Arturo Castillon, "Theses on the George Floyd Rebellion," June 24, 2020, https://illwill.com.

97 V. I. Lenin, *What Is to Be Done* (New York, 1969), p. 25.

98 Wohlleben, "Memes Without End."

99 Alain Badiou, *The Rebirth of History: Times of Riots and Uprisings* (London, 2021), p. 6.

100 All Gas No Brakes, "Minneapolis Protest."

Two: The Carceral State in Context

1 David Garland, ed., *Mass Imprisonment: Social Causes and Consequences* (London, 2021).

2 Prison Policy Initiative, "Mass Incarceration: The Whole Pie," March 24, 2020, www.prisonpolicy.org.

3 "Facts About Prisons and People in Prison" (2014), www.sentencingproject.org.

4 The Pew Center on the States, *One in 100: Behind Bars in America* (Washington, DC, 2008).

5 David Campbell, "Stick-Up on Rikers Island," May 1, 2020, www.hardcrackers.com.

6 Legal Aid Society, "Legal Aid Files Fourth Lawsuit to Free 100 Incarcerated New Yorkers at a High Risk of COVID-19 from Non-Criminal Technical Parole Violation Holds in Custody at Rikers Island," April 3, 2020, www.legalaidnyc.org.

7 Gregory Hooks and Wendy Sawyer, "Mass Incarceration, COVID-19 and Community Spread," December 2020, www.prisonpolicy.org.

8 Mark Neocleous, *The Fabrication of Order: A Critical Theory of Police Power* (London, 2000), p. xiv.

9 U.S. Bureau of Labor Statistics, "The Recession of 2007–9," February 2012, www.bls.gov.

10 See Leighton Walter Kille, "The Low-Wage Recovery: Industries and Jobs After the Great Recession," May 1, 2014, www.journalistresource.org. See also Olivier Coibion, Yuriy Gorodnichenko and Dmitri Koustas, "Amerisclerosis? The Puzzle of Rising U.S. Unemployment Persistence," Brookings Institute (Fall 2013), www.brookings.edu.

11 Aaron Benanav, *Automation and the Future of Work* (London, 2020); Jason Smith, *Smart Machines and Service Work: Automation in the Age of Stagnation* (London, 2020).

12 Chester Himes, *Blind Man With a Pistol* (New York, 1969), p. 235.

13 *The Kerner Report* (Princeton, NJ, 2016), p. 108.

14 George Russell, "The American Underclass: Destitute and Desperate in the Land of Plenty," *Time*, August 29, 1977.

15 William Julius Wilson, *The Declining Significance of Race* (Chicago, IL, 1978).

16 Barbara Jeanne Fields, "Slavery, Race and Ideology in the United States," *New Left Review*, I/181 (May/June 1990), pp. 95–118.

17 Anonymous seventeenth-century English poem cited by Peter Linebaugh in *Stop Thief: The Commons, Enclosures and Resistance* (Oakland, CA, 2014), p. 1.

18 Ibid.

19 Karl Marx, *Capital: A Critique of Political Economy*, vol. I: *The Process of Production of Capital* (New York, 1976), p. 896.

20 Karl Marx, "Critical Notes on the Article: 'The King of Prussia and Social Reform. By a Prussian'," in *Karl Marx and Frederick Engels: Collected Works* (New York, 1975), vol. III, pp. 189–206.

21 Ibid.

22 Frederick Engels, *The Conditions of the Working Class in England*, reissued edn (Oxford, 2009), p. 38.

23 Charles Dickens, *A Christmas Carol* (London, 1843), p. 13.

24 Marx, *Capital*, vol. I, pp. 283–306.

25 See the penitentiary's timeline at www.easternstate.org, accessed April 1, 2021.

26 Georg Rusche and Otto Kirchheimer, *Punishment and Social Structure* (New York, 1939).

27 W.E.B. Du Bois, *Black Reconstruction in America, 1860–1880* (New York, 1999), pp. 12, 55–83.

28 David M. Oshinsky, *Worse than Slavery: Parchman Farm and the Ordeal of Jim Crow Justice* (London, 1996), p. 18.

29 Keeanga-Yamahtta Taylor, *From #BlacklivesMatter to Black Liberation* (Chicago, IL, 2016), p. 109.

30 Ibid, pp. 109–10.

31 Du Bois, *Black Reconstruction*, p. 30.

32 Michelle Alexander, *The New Jim Crow: Mass Incarceration in the Age of Color Blindness* (New York, 2010), p. 29.

33 David J. Rothman, *Conscience and Convenience: The Asylum and Its Alternatives in Progressive America* (Boston, MA, 1979), p. 6.

34 Mark Neocleous, *The Fabrication of Social Order: A Critical Theory of Police Power* (London, 2000), p. 3.

35 Tyler Wall, "The Police Invention of Humanity: Notes on the 'Thin Blue Line'," *Crime, Media, Culture: An International Journal*, XVI/3 (December 2020), pp. 319–36.

36 Kristian Williams, *Our Enemies in Blue* (Oakland, CA, 2004).

37 Dian Million, "Policing the Rez: Keeping No Peace in Indian Country," *Social Justice*, XXVII/3 (2000), p. 102.

38 Noel Ignatiev, *How the Irish Became White* (London, 1995).

39 Simon Balto, *Occupied Territory: Policing Black Chicago from Red Summer to Black Power* (Chapel Hill, NC, 2000).

40 Stuart Hall et al., *Policing the Crisis: Mugging, the State, and Law and Order* (London, 1978), p. 394.

41 Michael Hirsch, "Remembering Robert Fitch," September 20, 2011, www.jacobinmag.com.

42 Fields, "Slavery, Race and Ideology in the United States."

43 Loren Goldner, "Race and Enlightenment," Part I: *Race Traitor*, 7 (1997); Part II: *Race Traitor*, 10 (1998).

44 See Noel Ignatiev's Foreword to Richard Wright, *12 Million Black Voices* (New York, 2002), pp. iv–vi.

45 Bruce Western and Becky Pettit, "Incarceration and Social Inequality," *Daedalus*, CXXXIX/3 (Summer 2010), pp. 8–19.

46 Angela Davis, *Are Prisons Obsolete?* (New York, 2011).

47 Loïc Wacquant, "The New 'Peculiar Institution': On the Prison as Surrogate Ghetto," *Theoretical Criminology*, IV/3 (August 2000), p. 72.

48 James Forman Jr., "Racial Critiques of Mass Incarceration: Beyond the New Jim Crow," *New York University Law Review*, LXXXVII/1 (April 2021), pp. 101–46.

49 Elizabeth Hinton, *From the War on Poverty to the War on Crime: The Making of Mass Incarceration in America* (Cambridge, MA, 2016).

50 Robert Brenner, *The Economics of Global Turbulence: The Advanced*

Capitalist Economies from Long Boom to Long Downturn, 1945–2005 (London, 2006), p. 113.

51 For a critique of the leftist tendency to dismiss crime, see Tony Platt "'Street Crime': A View from the Left," *Social Justice*, XL/1–2 (2014), pp. 216–30.

52 Adanar Usmani, "Did Liberals Give Us Mass Incarceration?," *Catalyst: A Journal of Theory and Strategy*, 1/3 (Fall 2017), pp. 169–83.

53 James Forman Jr., *Locking Up Our Own: Crime and Punishment in Black America* (New York, 2017).

54 Todd Clear, "Why America's Mass Incarceration Imperative Failed," April 29, 2014, www.pbs.org.

55 Todd Clear and Natasha Frost, *The Punishment Imperative: The Rise and Failure of Mass Incarceration in America* (New York, 2014), p. 33.

56 Ibid., p. 35.

57 Ibid.

58 Ruth Wilson Gilmore, *Golden Gulag: Prisons, Surplus, Crisis, and Opposition in Globalizing California* (Berkeley, CA, 2007), pp. 17, 24.

59 John Clegg and Adaner Usmani, "The Economic Origins of Mass Incarceration," *Catalyst: A Journal of Theory and Strategy*, III/3 (Fall 2019), pp. 9–53.

60 Jack Norton and David Stein, "Materializing Race: On Capitalism and Mass Incarceration," October 22, 2020, www.spectrejournal. com.

61 Du Bois, *Black Reconstruction*, p. 263.

62 See R. Subramanian et al., "Divided Justice: Trends in Black and White Jail Incarceration, 1990–2013," Vera Institute of Justice Safety and Justice Challenge (February 2018), www.vera.org. Data on Black/white disparities is complicated by the fact that many localities count Latinx as white (www.safetyandjusticechallenge. org). See also coverage in mainstream media, such as Keith Humphreys and Ekow N. Yankah, "Prisons are Getting Whiter: That's One Way Mass Incarceration Might End," February 26, 2021, www.washingtonpost.com.

63 Alexander, *The New Jim Crow*, p. 254.

64 James Forman Jr., "Racial Critiques of Mass Incarceration," p. 136.

Three: The Carceral State Today

1 See the Vera Institute of Justice's statement, "Ending Mass Incarceration," www.vera.org, accessed September 11, 2021.

2 The only exception in the data surveyed is Eastern European countries, which have experienced reduction in incarceration rates. See Helen Fair and Roy Walmsley, "World Population List," *Institute of Criminal Policy Research*, 12th edn, www.prisonstudies.org, accessed February 5, 2022.

3 Peter Wagner and Wendy Sawyer, "State of Incarceration: The Global Context 2018," Prison Policy Initiative, June 2018, www.prisonpolicy.org.
4 Sintia Radu, "Countries with the Highest Incarceration Rates," May 13, 2019, www.usnews.com.
5 Fair and Walmsley, "World Population List."
6 Ibid.
7 Victor L. Shammas, "The Rise of a More Punitive State: On the Attenuation of Norwegian Penal Exceptionalism in an Era of Welfare State Transformations," *Critical Criminology*, xxiv/1 (2016), pp. 57–74.
8 See Rona Lorimer, "Pity the Poor Police: New Laws to Back the Blue," May 2021, www.brooklynrail.org.
9 u.s. Department of Justice, Federal Bureau of Investigation, Uniform Crime Reporting, "Full Time Law Enforcement Employees by City and State" (2018), https://ucr.fbi.gov, accessed September 20, 2021.
10 Elle Let et al., "Racial Inequity in Fatal Police Shootings, 2005–2020," *Journal of Epidemiology and Community Health*, 75 (2021), pp. 394–7.
11 Pinar Bedirhanoğlu et al., *Turkey's New State in the Making: Transformations in Legality, Economy and Coercion* (London, 2020).
12 Carlos Conde, "Killings in the Philippines Up 50 Percent During the Pandemic," September 8, 2020, www.hrw.org.
13 Tim Henderson, "Felony Conviction Rates Have Risen Sharply, but Unevenly," January 2, 2018, www.pewtrusts.org.
14 The University of Georgia study does calculate Hispanic or other minority groups as a separate race. See ibid.
15 According to the last Census, African Americans comprise 13.4 percent of the u.s. population. Sarah K. S. Shannon et al., "The Growth, Scope, and Spatial Distribution of People with Felony Records in the United States, 1948–2010," *Demography*, liv/5 (October 2017), pp. 1795–818
16 Lucius Couloute, "Getting Back on Course: Educational Exclusion and Attainment Among Formerly Incarcerated People," October 2018, www.prisonpolicy.org.
17 Adam Looney and Nicholas Turner, "Work and Opportunity Before and After Incarceration," March 3, 2018, www.brookings.edu.
18 Karen Dolan and Jodi L. Carr, "The Poor Get Prison: The Alarming Spread of the Criminalization of Poverty," March 2015, www.ips-dc.org.
19 This is a central theme of Jackie Wang's *Carceral Capitalism* (Cambridge, ma, 2018).
20 Katherine Beckett and Naomi Murakawa, "Mapping the Shadow Carceral State: Toward an Institutionally Capacious Approach to Punishment," *Theoretical Criminology*, xvi/2 (May 2012), pp. 221–44.

21 Alexandra Natapoff, *Punishment Without Crime: How Our Massive Misdemeanor System Traps the Innocent and Makes America More Unequal* (New York, 2018).

22 Carlos Berdejó, "Criminalizing Race: Racial Disparities in Plea-Bargaining" (2018), https://lawdigitalcommons.bc.edu.

23 Alexandra Natapoff, "Criminal Municipal Courts," January 11, 2021, www.harvardlawreview.org.

24 Brendan Roediger, "Abolish Municipal Courts: A Response to Professor Natapoff," February 20, 2021, www.harvardlawreview.org.

25 U.S. Department of Justice, "Investigation of the Ferguson Police Department," March 4, 2015, www.justice.gov.

26 Alexandra Natapoff, "Criminal Municipal Courts."

27 Joseph Shapiro, "In Ferguson, Court Fines and Fees Fuel Anger," August 25, 2014, www.npr.org.

28 Colin Gordon and Clarissa Rile Hayward, "The Murder of Michael Brown," August 9, 2016, www.jacobinmag.com.

29 Fines and Fees Justice Center, "Tip of the Iceberg: How Much Criminal Justice Debt Does the U.S. Have?," April 21, 2021, https://finesandfeesjusticecenter.org.

30 Matthew Menendez and Lauren-Brooke Eisen, "The Steep Costs of Criminal Justice Fines and Fees," November 19, 2021, www.brennancenter.org.

31 Ibid.

32 Matthew Shaer, "How Cities Make Money by Fining the Poor," January 8, 2019, www.nytimes.com.

33 Chris Mai and Maria Rafael, "The High Price of Using Justice Fines and Fees to Fund Government in New York," December 2020, www.vera.org.

34 Alexes Harris et al., "United States Systems of Justice, Poverty and the Consequences of Non-Payment of Monetary Sanctions: Interviews from California, Georgia, Illinois, Minnesota, Missouri, Texas, New York, and Washington," Laura and John Arnold Foundation, November 2017, https://perma.cc/YJ3B-3PDK.

35 Mai and Rafael, "The High Price of Using Justice Fines and Fees to Fund Government in New York."

36 Harvard Law School, The National Criminal Justice Debt Initiative of the Criminal Justice Policy Program, The Criminal Justice Debt Reform Builder, "Poverty Penalties and Poverty Traps," www.cjdebtreform.org, accessed September 20, 2021.

37 Tracy Samilton, "ACLU Says 'Pay or Stay' Is Modern-Day Version of Debtors Prisons," September 29, 2014, www.michiganradio.org.

38 Sam Hotchkiss, "Rayshard Brooks: In His Own Words," June 17, 2020, www.reconnect.io.

39 Jake Horowitz, "1 in every 55 Adults Is on Probation or Parole," October 31, 2018, www.pewtrusts.org.

40 Human Rights Watch and ACLU, "Revoked: How Probation and Parole Feed Mass Incarceration," July 31, 2020, www.hrw.org.

41 Jake Horowitz, "Probation and Parole Systems Marked by High Stakes, Missed Opportunities," September 15, 2018, www.pewtrusts.org.

42 Michelle Phelps, "Mass Probation and Inequality," in *Handbook on Punishment Decisions: Locations of Disparity*, ed. Jeffrey T. Ulmer and Mindy S. Bradley (New York, 2018), p. 53.

43 Mack Finkel, "New Data: Low Incomes – but High Fees – for People on Probation," April 9, 2019, www.prisonpolicy.org.

44 Theresa Zhen and Brandon Greene, "Pay or Prey: How the Alameda County Criminal Justice System Extracts Wealth from Marginalized Communities," www.ebclc.org, accessed September 20, 2021.

45 Council of Economic Advisors, Issue Brief (December 2015), "Fines, Fees, and Bail: Payments in the Criminal Justice System That Disproportionately Impact the Poor," https://obamawhitehouse.archives.gov.

46 American Civil Liberties Union, "Brown vs Lexington, KY et al," July 22, 2017, www.aclu.org.

47 Vera Institute of Justice, "The Use of Fines as an Intermediate Sanction" (1991), www.vera.org.

48 Ibid., p. 5.

49 Wendy Sawyer and Peter Wagner, "Mass Incarceration: The Whole Pie, 2020," March 24, 2020, www.prisonpolicy.org.

50 Michael Waldman, "How Surcharges Punish the Poor: New York Must Combat Court Fees that Many Low-Income Residents Cannot Pay," February 2, 2019. www.brennancenter.org.

51 Reuben J. Miller, "Devolving the Carceral State: Race, Prisoner Reentry, and the Micro-Politics of Urban Poverty Management," *Punishment and Society*, XVI/3 (July 2014), pp. 305–35.

52 Maya Schenwar and Victoria Law, *Prison by Any Other Name: The Harmful Consequences of Popular Reforms* (New York, 2020), p. 40.

53 Georgia Department of Corrections, Reentry and Cognitive Programming, www.dcor.state.ga.us, accessed September 20, 2021.

54 Samantha Melamed, Dylan Purcell, and Chris A. Williams, "Everyone Is Detailed: How Probation Detainers Can Keep People Locked Up Indefinitely," December 27, 2019, www.inquirer.com.

55 Ibid.

56 Samantha Melamed and Dylan Purcell, "Living in Fear," October 24, 2019, www.inquirer.com.

57 Human Rights Watch, "Revoked: How Probation and Parole Feed Mass Incarceration in the United States," July 31, 2020, www.hrw.org.

58 Council of State Governments Justice Center (CSG), "Confined

and Costly: How Supervision Violations Are Filling Prisons and Burdening Budgets," June 18, 2019, https://csgjusticecenter.org.

59 Ibid.

60 Tommy Simmons, "Idaho Has the Highest Percentage Nationally of People in Prison Because of Supervision Violations," June 29, 2019, www.idahopress.com.

61 Vincent Schiraldi, "The Pennsylvania Community Corrections Story," April 25, 2018, https://justicelab.columbia.edu; Jarred Williams, Vincent Schiraldi, and Kendra Bradner, "The Wisconsin Community Corrections Story," January 22, 2019, https://justicelab.columbia.edu.

62 Julia Angwin et al., "Machine Bias," May 23, 2016, www.propublica.org.

63 Human Rights Watch and ACLU, "Revoked: How Probation and Parole Feed Mass Incarceration," July 31, 2020, www.hrw.org.

Four: The Limits of Reform in the Era of Austerity

1 Brendan Morrow, "Joe Biden: Do I Look Like a Radical Socialist with a Soft Spot for Rioters, Really?," August 31, 2020, www.theweek.com.

2 "Onward Barbarians," May 26, 2021, https://endnotes.org.uk.

3 William I. Robinson, The Global Police State (London, 2020).

4 David Ranney, New World Disorder: The Decline of U.S. Power (North Charleston, SC, 2014), pp. 9–10.

5 Byron Tao, "Republican National Committee Backs Overhaul of Criminal Justice System," April 22, 2016, www.wsj.com.

6 Dan Berger, "Social Movements and Mass Incarceration," Souls: A Critical Journal of Black Politics, Culture, and Society, XV/1–2 (2013), pp. 3–18: p. 14.

7 Brown vs Plata, 131 S. Ct. 1910 (2011).

8 Ruth Gilmore and Craig Gilmore, "Beyond Bratton," in Policing the Planet: Why the Policing Crisis Led to Black Lives Matter, ed. Jordan P. Camp and Christina Heatherton (London and New York, 2016).

9 Kay Whitlock and Nancy A. Heitzeg, Carceral Con: The Deceptive Terrain of Criminal Justice Reform (Oakland, CA, 2021).

10 Jacob Kang-Brown and Jack Norton, "Funding Jail Expansion in California's Central Valley," October 8, 2020, www.vera.org.

11 Hadar Aviram, Cheap on Crime: Recession-Era Politics and the Transformation of American Punishment (Oakland, CA, 2015), p. 11.

12 Hadar Aviram, "The Correctional Hunger Games: Understanding Realignment in the Context of the Great Recession," ANNALS of the American Academy of Political and Social Science, DCLXIV/1 (March 2016), p. 263.

13 David Rothman, The Discovery of the Asylum (New York, 1971), p. 295.

14 Thomas Mathiesen, The Politics of Abolition (Hoboken, NY, 1974).

15 Michel Foucault, *Discipline and Punish: The Birth of the Prison* (New York, 1977).

16 Loïc Wacquant, "Deadly Symbiosis: When Ghetto and Prison Meet and Mesh," *Punishment and Society*, III/1 (January 2001), p. 109.

17 "Attica: The Official Report of the New York State Special Commission on Attica" (New York, 1972), p. xii, at https://nysl.ptfs. com, accessed February 23, 2021.

18 Andrew Scull, *Decarceration: Community Treatment and the Deviant: A Radical View* (Englewood Cliffs, NJ, 1977).

19 Joshua Dubler and Vincent Lloyd, "Think Prison Abolition in America Is Impossible? It Once Felt Inevitable," May 18, 2018, www.theguardian.com.

20 Marie Gottschalk, "The Folly of Neoliberal Prison Reform," June 8, 2015, www.bostonreview.net.

21 U.S. Bureau of Justice Statistics, "Prisoners in 2014," September 2015, p. 16, www.bjs.ojp.gov; Ryan King et al., "How to Reduce the Federal Prison Population" (2015), www.urban.org.

22 Under Obama, federal authorities exercised restraint in prosecution of drugs in states where it was legal.

23 Ed Chung, "Smart on Crime: An Alternative to the Tough vs Soft Debate," May 12, 2017, www.americanprogress.org.

24 Kamala Harris, *Smart on Crime: A Career Prosecutor's Plan to Make Us Safer* (San Francisco, CA, 2008).

25 U.S. Department of Justice, "Smart on Crime: Reforming the Criminal Justice System for the 21st Century," August 12, 2013, www.justice.gov.

26 As cited in Shane Bauer, "How Conservatives Learned to Love Prison Reform," March/April 2014, www.motherjones.com.

27 Newt Gingrich and Pat Nolan, "Don't Train Kids to Be Felons in Adult Jails," June 1, 2016, www.theadvocate.com.

28 The Rick Perry Report Card, June 10, 2014, www.texasmonthly.com.

29 Marie Gottschalk, "Tougher than the Rest: No Criminal Justice Reform 'Miracle' in Texas," January 1, 2021, www.prisonlegalnews.org.

30 See the 'About' section at www.rightoncrime.com, accessed September 20, 2021.

31 The American Civil Liberties Union, "Smart Reform Is Possible: States Reducing Incarceration Rates and Costs While Protecting Communities," August 2011, www.aclu.org.

32 Gottschalk, "Tougher than the Rest."

33 Marie Gottschalk, *Caught: The Prison State and the Lockdown of American Politics* (Princeton, NJ, 2015), p. 41.

34 Ibid.; Hadar Aviram, *Cheap on Crime: Recession Era Politics and the Transformation of American Punishment* (Oakland, CA, 2015); Ruth Wilson Gilmore, "The Worrying State of the Anti-Prison Movement" (2015), www.socialjusticejournal.org; Sarah Cate and Daniel HoSang,

"The Better Way to Fight Crime: Why Fiscal Arguments Do Not Constrain the Fiscal State," *Theoretical Criminology*, XXII/2 (May 2018), pp. 169–88; Christopher Seeds, "Bifurcation Nation: American Penal Policy in Late Mass Incarceration," *Punishment and Society*, XIX/5 (December 2017), pp. 590–610.

35 U.S. Federal Bureau of Prisons, "An Overview of the First Step Act," www.bop.gov, accessed September 1, 2022.

36 Marie Gottschalk, "Did You Really Think Trump Was Going to Help End the Carceral State?," March 9, 2019, www.jacobinmag.com.

37 Josh Barro, "New York's Most Expensive Apartments Are Jail Cells," August 23, 2013, www.businessinsider.com.

38 Jennifer Gonnerman, "Before the Law," September 29, 2014, www.newyorker.com.

39 Raven Rakia and Ashoka Jegroo, "How the Push to Close Rikers Went from No Jails to New Jails," May 29, 2018, https://theappeal. org.

40 The Independent Commission on New York City Criminal Justice and Incarceration Reform [Lippman Commission], *A More Just City* (New York, 2017); Van Alen Institute and Lippman Commission, *Justice in Design: Towards a Healthier and More Just New York City Jail System* (New York, 2017); Lippman Commission, *A More Just City: One Year Forward* (New York, 2018); Michael Jacobson et al., "Beyond the Island: Changing the Culture of New York City Jails," *Fordham Urban Law Journal*, XLV/2 (2018), pp. 373–436; Janos Marton "#CLOSErikers: The Campaign to Transform New York City's Criminal Justice System," *Fordham Urban Law Journal*, XLV/2 (2018), pp. 499–570.

41 Timothy Williams, "The City Withdraws Its Proposal for a $375 Million Jail in the South Bronx," March 8, 2008, www.nytimes.com.

42 Zhandarka Kurti and Jarrod Shanahan, "Carceral Non-Profits and the Limits of Prison Reform," ACME: *Journal for Critical Geographies*, XX/5 (2022), pp. 597–617.

43 James Kilgore, "Repackaging Mass Incarceration," June 6, 2014, www.counterpunch.org.

44 Soffiyah Elijah, "'No New Jails' Means the Same Old Jails," October 11, 2019, www.nydailynews.com.

45 This is the ethic that guides the Alternative to Incarceration Initiative of the Los Angeles Chief Executive Office. See https://ceo.lacounty.gov/ati, accessed February 1, 2022.

46 Lauren Lee White, "We Didn't Stop: The Los Angeles Abolition Coalition That's Racking Up Victories," April 9, 2021, www.theguardian.com.

47 Zhandarka Kurti and Jarrod Shanahan, "Rebranding Mass Incarceration: The Lippman Commission and Carceral Devolution in New York City," *Social Justice*, XLV/2–3 (2018), pp. 25–49.

48 Brendan McQuade, *Pacifying the Homeland: Intelligence Fusion and Mass Supervision* (Oakland, CA, 2019), p. 167.

49 Jasmine Hess and Jack Norton, "Mass Incarceration Is a Rural Problem, Too," January 25, 2020, www.jacobinmag.com.

50 Jacob-Brown and Ram Subramanian, "Out of Sight: The Growth of Jails in Rural America," June 2017, www.vera.org.

Five: "Defund the Police": At the Crossroads of Revolution and Reform

1 Rebecca Tan et al., "Protesters Paint 'Defund the Police' Right Next to DC's 'Black Lives Matter' Mural," June 7, 2020, www.washingtonpost.com.

2 Karl Marx and Friedrich Engels, *Manifesto of the Communist Party* (New York, 1955), p. 13.

3 Mariame Kaba, "Yes We Mean Literally Abolish the Police," June 12, 2020, www.nytimes.com.

4 "'I Want Us to Dream a Little Bigger': Noname and Mariame Kaba on Art and Abolition," December 19, 2020, www.npr.org.

5 Angela Davis, speech delivered at the Embassy Auditorium, June 9, 1972, at http://americanradioworks.publicradio.org/ features/blackspeech/adavis.html, accessed October 3, 2021.

6 See Albert Woodfox, *Solitary: Unbroken by Four Decades in Solitary Confinement, My Story of Transformation and Hope* (New York, 2019).

7 Toussaint Losier, "Against 'Law and Order' Lockup: The 1970 NYC Jail Rebellions," *Race and Class*, LIX/1 (July–September 2017), pp. 3–35; Orisanmi Burton, "Organized Disorder: The New York City Jail Rebellion of 1970," *Black Scholar: Journal of Black Studies and Research*, XLVIII/4 (Winter 2018), pp. 28–42.

8 Beth Richie, *Arrested Justice: Black Women, Violence, and America's Prison Nation* (New York, 2012).

9 Emily L. Thuma, *All Our Trials: Prisons, Policing, and the Feminist Fight to End Violence* (Urbana, IL, 2009), p. 5.

10 Angela Davis, "Joan Little: The Dialects of Rape," *Ms. Magazine* (June 1975), www.overthrowpalace.home.blog, accessed February 2021.

11 As Thuma points out, the events at Bedford—namely, the defense of the "Mateawan sisters"—led the group to change its name from Women Against Prisons to Women Free Women in Prison. Thuma, *All Our Trials*, p. 96.

12 Adrienne Brown, "An Interview with Activists at the Prison Moratorium Project," June 22, 2005, https://grist.org.

13 Mike Davis, "Hell Factories in the Field: A Prison-Industrial Complex," *The Nation* (February 1995), pp. 229–34; Eric Schlosser, "The Prison-Industrial Complex," *The Atlantic* (December 1998), pp. 51–77; Angela Davis, "Masked Racism: Reflections on the Prison

Industrial Complex," *ColorLines* (Fall 1998), pp. 1–4. We have elected not to use the term "prison industrial complex," due to the persistent incorrect belief among young students of the U.S. carceral system that prisoner labor furnishes a profitable industry that generates profit on top of the costs of incarceration. Our decision also draws upon the scholarship of abolitionists who have looked at "alternatives to incarceration" as part and parcel of the prison system.

14 See especially Angela Davis, *Abolition Democracy: Beyond Empire, Prisons, and Torture* (Boston, MA, 2005).

15 See Ruth Wilson Gilmore, *Golden Gulag: Prisons, Surplus, Crisis, and Opposition in Globalizing California* (Berkeley, CA, 2007).

16 For an overview of the group's first decade, see CR10 Publications Collective, *Abolition Now: Ten Years of Strategy and Struggle Against the Prison Industrial Complex* (Oakland, CA, 2008).

17 "INCITE! History," www.incite-national.org, accessed January 15, 2021.

18 Prison Research Education Action, *Instead of Prisons: A Handbook for Abolitionists* (Syracuse, NY, 1976).

19 INCITE!, *The Revolution Will Not Be Funded: Beyond the Non-Profit Industrial Complex* (Boston, MA, 2007).

20 Dan Berger, Mariame Kaba, and David Stein, "What Abolitionists Do," August 24, 2017, www.jacobinmag.com.

21 Zhandarka Kurti and Jarrod Shanahan, "Carceral Non-Profits and the Limits of Prison Reform," ACME: *Journal for Critical Geographies*, xx/6 (2021), pp. 597–617.

22 No New Jails NYC, *Close Rikers Now, We Keep Us Safe*, https://keyboard-sailfish-lnbg.squarespace.com, accessed October 31, 2021.

23 Adrian Wohlleben, "Memes Without End," May 16, 2021, https://illwill.com.

24 Fola Akinnibi, Sarah Holder, and Christopher Cannon, "Cities Say They Want to Defund the Police. Their Budgets Say Otherwise," January 12, 2021, www.bloomberg.com.

25 "Choosing Real Safety: A Historic Declaration to Divest from Policing and Prisons and Build Safer Communities for All," www.choosingrealsafety.com, accessed August 2021.

26 Camille E.S.A. Acey, "This Is an Illogical Statement: Dangerous Trends in Anti-Prison Activism," *Social Justice*, XXVII/3 (Fall 2000), pp. 206–11.

27 Michel Foucault, *Discipline and Punish: The Birth of the Prison* (New York, 1977), p. 228.

28 Kay Gabriel, "Defund Is a Strategy," June 7, 2021, www.versobooks.com.

29 Pilar Maschi and Jarrod Shanahan, "There Are Abolitionists All Around Us," Winter 2020, https://communemag.com.

30 Alex Vitale, *The End of Policing* (London, 2017).
31 Leah Donnella, "How Much Do We Need the Police," June 3, 2020, www.npr.org.
32 Staughton Lynd and Daniel Gross, *Labor Law for the Rank-and-Filer: Building Solidarity While Staying Clear of the Law* (Oakland, CA, 2008), p. 15.
33 Steve Jenkins, "Organizing, Advocacy, and Member Power," *WorkingUSA*, VI/2 (Fall 2002), pp. 56–89.
34 Jocelyn Cohn and James Frey, "Against Transparency," November 6, 2012, www.libcom.org.
35 Jennifer R. Wolch, *The Shadow State: Government and Voluntary Sector in Transition* (New York, 1990).
36 Karl Marx, *Capital: A Critique of Political Economy*, vol. III: *The Process of Capitalist Production as a Whole* (New York, 1981), p. 736.
37 Maya Schenwar and Victoria Law, *Prison by Any Other Name: The Harmful Consequences of Popular Reforms* (New York, 2020), p. 237.
38 Noel Ignatiev, "The Point Is Not to Interpret Whiteness but to Abolish It" [1997], September 16, 2019, https://blog.pmpress.org.
39 C.L.R. James, *Notes on Dialectics: Hegel, Marx, Lenin* [1969] (Westport, CT, 1980), p. 99.
40 C.L.R. James, *American Civilization* (Cambridge, MA, 1993), p. 168.
41 Joy James, "Airbrushing Revolution for the Sake of Abolition," Black Perspectives, July 20, 2020, www.aaihs.org.
42 DSA Emerge, "The Abolitionist Horizon: Building a World Without Police or Prisons," June 24, 2020, https://dsaemerge.org.
43 Gabriel, "Defund Is a Strategy."
44 Amna Akbar, "The Left Is Remaking the World," July 11, 2020, www.nytimes.com.
45 Tobi Haslett, "Magic Actions," May 7, 2021, www.nplusonemag.com.
46 DSA Emerge, "The Abolitionist Horizon."
47 Shemon Salam, "The Rise of Black Counter-Insurgency," July 30, 2020, https://illwill.com.
48 Angela Davis, *Abolition Democracy* (Oakland, CA, 2005), pp. 69, 91–3.
49 Noel Ignatiev, "The American Blindspot: Reconstruction According to Eric Foner and W.E.B. Du Bois," *Labour/Le Travail*, XXXI (Spring 1993), pp. 243–51.
50 Revolutionary Abolitionist Movement, *Burn Down the American Plantation: Call for a Revolutionary Abolitionist Movement* (New York, 2017).
51 H8ers: An Insurrectionary Journal from North Texas (2020), https://haters.noblogs.org.
52 SM28 Collective, "The Spirit of May 28th," July 8, 2021, https://fighttowin.noblogs.org.
53 Salam, "Black Counter-Insurgency."

54 Karl Marx, "Contribution to the Critique of Hegel's Philosophy of Law: Introduction," in *Karl Marx and Frederick Engels* (New York, 1975), vol. III, p. 182.

Afterword

1 Melissa Alonzo and Josh Campbell, "Minneapolis Police Officers Pen Open Letter Condemning Former Officer Derek Chauvin," June 13, 2020, www.cnn.com.
2 Janelle Griffith, "Derek Chauvin 'Absolutely' Violated Policy, Minneapolis Police Chief Testifies," April 5, 2021, www.nbc.com.
3 Anonymous, "The Only Way Out Is Always Through the Police: A History of the Rise and Fall of the 2020 New York Riots," July 15, 2021, www.itsgoingdown.org.